THE MASTERS PLAN FOR MAKING DISCIPLES

How every Christian can be an effective witness through an enabling church

WIN ARN
CHARLES ARN

Now . . . an effective seminar and the practical tools to see the insights of THE MASTER'S PLAN move from the pages of this book to the very heartbeat of your church and its members!

Write for complete information and a descriptive brochure to:

Church Growth
709 E. Colorado Blvd. Suite #150
Pasadena, CA 91101

© Copyright 1982 by Church Growth Press
709 E. Colorado Blvd., Suite #150, Pasadena, CA 91101

Library of Congress Catalog Card No. 81-69766
ISBN 0-934408-05-X
Second printing 1982
Third printing 1983
Fourth printing 1983

Printed in the U.S.A.

In Appreciation

We want to acknowledge and appreciate the following people for their contributions to this book:

Carroll Nyquist, for his insights which have brought a depth and breadth to the concepts of The Master's Plan, and for his creation of "Chuck Bradley," a character who has helped us all to see ourselves a little more clearly;

Margaret Self, for her research and analysis of the principles of The Master's Plan;

Donald McGavran, for his original identification of the webs principle that is an important part of The Master's Plan.

Contents

Introduction

In the beginning the early church grew . . . with mega power!

The events are recorded in the book of The Acts . . . from 12 . . . to 120 . . . to 3000 . . . to 5000 . . . from addition to multiplication . . . to entire communities turning to the Lord. Then off on its globe-circling mission—a mission given by the Head of the Church, Jesus Christ, to disciple the many diverse peoples who make up the human family.

Through the centuries, the Church has grown . . . grown among alien cultures . . . grown among hostile religions . . . grown among both primitive and sophisticated peoples. The Church has triumphed over traitors, persecution, famine, and sword.

The church's one foundation is Jesus Christ her Lord;
She is His new creation, by water and the Word:
From heaven He came and sought her, to be His holy bride;
With His own blood He bought her, and for her life He died.

Elect from every nation, yet one o'er all the earth,
Her charter of salvation, one Lord, one faith, one birth;
One holy name she blesses, partakes one holy food,
And to one hope she presses, with every grace endued.

'Mid toil and tribulation, and tumult of her war,
She waits the consumation of peace forevermore;
Till with the vision glorious her longing eyes are blest,
And the great Church victorious shall be the Church at rest.

Samuel J. Stone

The Church of Jesus Christ has grown, and continues to grow, to complete the task . . . a task yet unfinished.

As the Church has grown in innumerable ways and places, there has always been one way it has grown better, faster, and stronger than any other. From its beginning, through the centuries till today, one unique way has been more responsible for the Church's growth than any other. It is about this way—and the important implications it has for you and your church—that this book was written.

What About Today? The State of Evangelism

But while the Church has grown—and there are more Christians today than ever before in the history of the world—there is still a vast unfinished task. Throughout the world, three out of every four people have yet to believe. In the United States, out of a population of approximately 226 million, there are nearly 165 million pagans or marginal Christians ("Christians" in name only). Around every church in every community, there are winnable people waiting to be won. In fact, never in history has the world-wide potential for evangelism and church growth been greater. Yet . . . that one way which God has used and blessed so greatly through the centuries seems to be strangely lacking in modern evangelistic endeavors.

A closer look at the state of evangelism today is in order. Evangelism is not well. In fact, the lack of results through intentional evangelism, compared to the task yet to be accomplished in America today, should cause Christians both apprehension and concern. And it is as a direct result of the impotency in disciple-making today that this book and supportive material have been researched and developed.

The Lord's words to His followers two thousand years ago remain unchanged for His followers today. His commands have not been updated, nor have they been revoked. "Go therefore and make disciples of all nations, baptizing them in the name of the Father and the Son and the Holy Spirit, teaching them to observe all that I have commanded you;

and lo, I am with you always even to the end of the age."[1]

But what about today? How do 20th century Christians view this biblical mandate? Is the goal of making disciples still at the center of the activities and prayers of Christ's Church?

During the last nine years, in traveling across America ministering in churches, conducting seminars, holding consultations, conferring with church leaders, discussing with laity, it has been our privilege to "feel the pulse" of evangelism today. Based on our wide experience across the Protestant denominational spectrum, we have observed some important characteristics of evangelism in America.

1. Reaching non-Christians is a low priority for most congregations. What was once the heartbeat of the entire church, particularly the early church, has diminished enormously as a priority in the minds of its members. What was once an important criteria for success[2] has diminished to merely one item (and not a particularly important one) on the church's busy agenda. Church activities have become increasingly inward-focused. Events planned, money raised and spent, roles and jobs created are conducted primarily as a service to members and for maintenance of the organization.

Evangelistic activities, visitation programs, and witness training hold little enticement for the average congregation. Outreach functions are relegated to a small and usually impotent committee. "Making disciples" has become, in most congregations, a compartmentalized function, isolated from the mainstream of church thinking and life.

Contributing to this decline in priority is the fact that many laity and clergy no longer see the church as the instrument to reach the world. They believe, mistakenly, that the television and radio air waves, the nation-wide media blitzes, or the mass-evangelism rallies are the only effective way to respond to the Great Commission and reach the millions of unreached. Few perceive their own congregation as having the potential for being God's instrument to reach their community.

2. Reaching non-Christians is a low priority for most individual Christians. Very few lay people feel able to effectively share their faith. When asked why they are a Christian and church member, many can mumble little more than, "Well, it's a good thing to be." Not that they aren't enthusiastic about the reality of Christ in their life, they have just never been helped to communicate it. Most Christians today lack the training which would enable them to share what Christ means to them with a non-Christian in a natural, effective way.

While many laity feel inadequate in expressing their Christian beliefs, some are even unsure of what they *do* believe. Christian "in name only" typifies nearly one half of all the people today who call themselves "Christians."

3. The biblical concept of "lostness" has disappeared from the conscience of most churches and most Christians. In our modern culture, the understanding of what was once a theological imperative—of people outside Christ being eternally lost—has changed in the minds of many believers. The reasons behind this are varied and complex. They may range from a world influenced primarily by "situation ethics" to a general erosion of confidence in the Scripture. However, many believers tend to perceive "lostness" only in a sociological dimension, neglecting the spiritual dimension. For many, "lostness" has little to do with the Biblical concept of eternal separation from God.

Little remains of the first-century Christian's burning conviction that without Christ, every person is forever lost. Nor is there that fervent zeal for non-Christian friends and relatives which swept across America as great evangelists graphically portrayed the terrifying damnation of a God-less eternity. Today's Christians are not convinced of the reality of this foundational concept of Christianity.

4. Most evangelism methods are relatively ineffective in making disciples. The "bottom line" following evangelism efforts is—does the church grow? In many churches there are more people leaving through the "back door" of natural attrition (transfer, death, reversion, etc.) than there are new Christians coming in the "front door" as a result of evangelism programs. That is not to say that their churches aren't growing—some are. They just aren't growing as a result of the evangelism program.

Local congregations, sincere in their efforts to reach out with the Gospel, often "import" a program or formula that has seemingly been successful in other churches. The methods widely used often attempt to compact a life-transforming Gospel presentation into a 15-minute or less visitation call. In the process, little consideration is given to the unique needs of the individual. The non-Christian has a very limited opportunity to dialogue about the consequences of this major step of faith. No significant relationships are established. Non-Christians seldom, if ever, have a chance to observe the realities of Christ in the lives of Christians. And often there is no effective plan for the new convert to become incorporated into the life of the local congregation.[3] Indeed some evangelism methods encourage callers not to even mention the church in their conversation.

5. Evangelism focuses on decision-making rather than disciple-making. Most mass and local church evangelism approaches today have a significant common shortcoming. Attention is centered, and success judged around the goal of getting a "decision." That brief verbal commitment is seen as the ultimate response to the Great Commission. Unfortunately, there is often a great gap between "getting a decision" and "making a disciple." A "disciple" suggests a commitment, incorporation into the Body, then an ongoing, reproductive life-style as a follower of Christ. An analysis of many church training programs and para-church crusades in America today indicates that the bottom line for evangelism is the number of decisions recorded. This "decision-making" mentality may actually be one of the reasons national church membership continues to decline, in relation to population growth, in spite of so much being said and done in mass evangelism, media evangelism, evangelism training, and evangelism conferences.

6. Making disciples is interpreted to mean only spiritual growth. In the Great Commission, Jesus makes clear that the command to "go and make disciples" includes the concept of *winning*. Today the term "discipling" has almost universally evolved to mean the process of spiritual perfecting—tutoring, learning, growing, maturing. Few "discipling" programs in churches today accurately reflect Christ's vision to make disciples, or measure their success on the basis of new disciples they produce.

While the concept of spiritual maturation is unquestionably important, an exclusive emphasis on spiritual growth often serves as an undesirable magnet pulling a Christian's focus increasingly inward, as the concern for those outside the Body of Christ progressively decreases.[4] In such a self-centered environment, the goal of fulfilling the Lord's Great Commission moves lower and lower as a priority.

7. Evangelism methods have become simplistic. There is strong research evidence to indicate that new Christians who accept Christ and continue as responsible church members first perceive the Gospel message in terms of its relevance to their own lives. Evangelism training which relies on "canned" presentations, memorized testimonies, and universal spiritual dictums has difficulty responding to the unique needs of the non-Christian in terms of his/her day-to-day experience and the resources available in Christ.

New Christians who continue as responsible church members have first perceived the Gospel message in terms of its unique application to their own lives, situations, and problems. Dr. Arthur Glasser observes, "People today must see Jesus Christ as the liberator from injustice, transformer of human culture, as well as personal Savior of the human heart."[5]

8. Evangelism is much discussed but little

practiced. The following parable reprinted from CHURCH GROWTH: AMERICA magazine, speaks insightfully of the problem of much talk but little effective action:

"Now it came to pass that a group existed who called themselves fishermen. And lo, there were many fish in the waters all around. In fact, the whole area was surrounded by streams and lakes filled with fish. And the fish were hungry.

"Week after week, month after month, and year after year these, who called themselves fishermen, met in meetings and talked about their call to go about fishing.

"Continually they searched for new and better methods of fishing and for new and better definitions of fishing. They sponsored costly nationwide and worldwide congresses to discuss fishing and to promote fishing and hear about all the ways of fishing, such as the new fishing equipment, fish calls, and whether any new bait was discovered.

"These fishermen built large, beautiful buildings called 'Fishing Headquarters.' The plea was that everyone should be a fisherman and every fisherman should fish. One thing they didn't do, however; they didn't fish.

"All the fishermen seemed to agree that what is needed is a board which could challenge fishermen to be faithful in fishing. The board was formed by those who had the great vision and courage to speak about fishing, to define fishing, and to promote the idea of fishing in far-away streams and lakes where many other fish of different colors lived.

"Large, elaborate, and expensive training centers were built whose purpose was to teach fishermen how to fish. Those who taught had doctorates in fishology. But the teachers did not fish. They only taught fishing.

"Some spent much study and travel to learn the history of fishing and to see far-away places where the founding fathers did great fishing in the centuries past. They lauded the faithful fishermen of years before who handed down the idea of fishing.

"Many who felt the call to be fishermen responded. They were commissioned and sent to fish. And they went off to foreign lands . . . to teach fishing.

"Now it's true that many of the fishermen sacrificed and put up with all kinds of difficulties. Some lived near the water and bore the smell of dead fish every day. They received the ridicule of some who made fun of their fishermen's clubs. They anguished over those who were not committed enough to attend the weekly meetings to talk about fishing. After all, were they not following the Master who said, 'Follow me, and I will make you fishers of men?'

"Imagine how hurt some were when one day a person suggested that those who don't catch fish were really not fishermen, no matter how much they claimed to be. Yet it did sound correct. Is a person a fisherman if year after year he/she never catches a fish? Is one following if he/she isn't fishing?"[6]

So What About Today?

How does this present "state of evangelism" compare to the New Testament "state of evangelism"? Interestingly, there were significant differences in the early church . . .

1. Reaching non-Christians was a high priority for the church. Indeed the very "call to arms" of Christ for His Church was to reach out and make disciples.

2. Reaching non-Christians was a high priority for individual Christians. It was an assumption that every Christian was to be a committed witness to Christ's love.

3. The concept of "lostness" was foremost in the minds of Christians and churches. Christians believed wholeheartedly that Jesus Christ was *the* way, the truth, and the life.

4. Evangelism methods were designed to make disciples. Peter . . . Paul . . . Philip . . . Barnabas . . . Mark . . . the success of their endeavors was measured by the growth of the church and new disciples. Throughout the book of Acts, references are found pointing to the growth of the church and the multiplication of disciples.

5. Evangelism focused on disciple-making not decision-

making. Nowhere in Scripture is the concept of "decisions" found. The bottom line was a transformed life and an active Christian—a disciple.

6. Making disciples meant spiritual growth and making new disciples. Christ said it best when he said to go and baptize new disciples, and then to teach them all he had told them. First reaching, then teaching . . . the two went hand in hand.

7. Evangelism methods presented the whole Gospel and its implications. When people made a Christian commitment, they knew the implications and the potential price they might have to pay.

8. Evangelism was the priority of the church. And they were his witnesses in Jerusalem, Judea, Samaria, and to the uttermost parts of their world.

Are we, as Christians, simply to wait for our Lord's return with no concern for those people still outside of God's family? Of course not! Disciples are commissioned . . . as much today as they were by Christ Himself. What is more, the harvest fields are ripe across North America . . . and throughout the world. Within the last few years a great spiritual awakening has begun. Christian concepts are receiving high visibility and credibility as never before. Awareness and receptivity are increasing. Old frustrations resulting from years of failure are bringing a new and desperate plea: "Show us a better way!"

Are churches catching the vision and seizing the opportunities for making disciples? Growth is indeed occurring in some congregations where members are actively involved in sharing God's love and building His Body. Excitement and enthusiasm are permeating churches where new Christians are being lovingly incorporated into the fellowship of believers.

God is not going to be defeated! Jesus Christ is not powerless! God is the Father Almighty. The Church has abundant resources and excellencies, and evidences a strength and goodness no other organization dares to dream of. The facts indicate that the church is expanding and will continue to do so.

But how can more Christians and more churches respond to this opportunity for making disciples? The future is bright for any church dedicated to the task of fulfilling the Great Commission. *But there must be a fresh beginning!* Old methods have not and will not bring in the catch that is waiting just outside the boat. There is a better way, a creative and enjoyable and effective way for you and your church to bring in a net that will be full beyond your most fervent prayers and greatest expectations . . .

We believe the strategy reviewed in this text uses the powerful principles of disciple-making exemplified and called for by our own Master. *The Master's Plan* seeks to identify, illustrate, explain, and apply for you and your church both principles and practices which have and will continue to produce abundant results in the lives of individuals and churches . . . for the glory of God and the growth of His Church!

Footnotes

1. Matthew 28:19,20
2. See Acts 1:15, 2:41, 2:47, 4:4, 5:14, 6:1, 6:7, 9:31, 11:21, 16:5, 21:20
3. Samuel Southard, *Pastoral Evangelism* (Atlanta: John Knox Press, 1981), pp. 138,139.
4. Charles Arn, Donald McGavran, Win Arn, *Growth: A New Vision for the Sunday School* (Pasadena: Church Growth Press, 1980), p. 40.
5. Arthur Glasser, *Why Church Growth* (Christian Communication: Part II, N.D.).
6. Win Arn, *The Pastor's Church Growth Handbook* (Pasadena: Church Growth Press, 1979), pp. 151-154.

The Master's Plan— Making Disciples

Wearily Chuck Bradley turned to his wife. "Diane, I'm not going. . .and that's final!"

"But, Chuck, I promised you'd go with me," replied Diane.

"Don't I have the right to make up my own mind?"

"Well, sure you do, sweetheart, but I just assumed you'd be interested in learning more about evangelism."

"Please, Diane, don't try to make me feel guilty!"

"But just think how it will look if I go alone. People will say, 'Chuck Bradley doesn't care about sharing his faith.' "

Chuck did not like the direction this conversation was taking. "Diane, you know that's not true. I do care about evangelism, as much as anybody. I just don't care about another 'witnessing seminar'."

"But, Chuck, Pastor Austin said this would be different."

"Well, of course he'd say that. Diane, I'm just tired of trying to learn one new method after another for witnessing. You'd think we were some kind of door-to-door salesmen."

"But, Chuck, you do believe that Christians ought to share their faith?"

"You know I do. . .but I'm just not sure Jesus is supposed to be marketed by people acting like Fuller brushmen and Avon ladies. Besides, I haven't had much success with those kinds of methods anyway. Remember the summer we went camping. . .and I tried out my new witnessing training? Why,

"Remember the summer we went camping . . . and I tried out my new witnessing training," Chuck retorted.

a couple of people even agreed to make a decision. And then. . ."

Diane interrupted. "Yes, Chuck, I know. . .You heard one of them say later that the way to get rid of those missionary types was to say 'Yes' so they'll soon go away and leave you alone."

"I really heard that Diane."

"Chuck, a few bad experiences shouldn't give you the right to stop witnessing."

"You're absolutely right, Diane. But at this moment I have a very hard time believing that anything I say. . .as a witness. . .will really make a difference in another person's life."

"But if you went with me tonight. . .maybe you'd learn something that would help," pleaded Diane.

"No, Diane. When it comes to witnessing, I feel just like those disciples who fished all night and caught absolutely nothing!"

▶◀◆▶◀◆▶◀◉▶◀◆▶◀◆▶◀

How do you feel about witnessing? Or sharing your faith? There are a lot of Christians who feel like Chuck. Although they believe in evangelism, their personal efforts have had little or no results. Like the disciples, they have "fished all night and caught nothing."

But remember that's not the end of the story. Let's refresh our memories.. . .

The first rays of a new morning sun peek over the eastern sunburned hills. Stretching out for miles below lies a quiet, mirror-like blue lake. A few hundred yards offshore a solitary boat appears fastened to the still surface. Periodically one of the two figures in the twenty-foot wooden boat stands and stretches. The motionless air carries the occasional morning wake-up call of a rooster across the water.

Finally, the men begin to pull in their nets, causing ripples of disturbed water to ring their way from the boat toward shore. The water from wet nets being pulled to the surface breaks the morning silence as the fishermen eagerly search their nets for the product of their labors from the long night. But as the last of the empty nets pile onto the boat bottom, they discouragingly reach for the oars. Another wasted night.

"How's the fishing?" a man calls from shore.

After a pause, a frustrated voice replies, "Nothing. Absolutely nothing!"

"Throw your nets on the other side of the boat," orders the man on shore.

"But we've fished all night." Then, after a long pause, and sensing an authority in the voice, the fisherman responds, "All right, but only once more . . ."

A short time later, after again letting out their nets into the same water, shouts of excitement ring out. Calls for help sound from the boat . . .help to bring in the nets which are so full they are beginning to break!

What a moment that must have been! Peter and Andrew trying desperately to bring in the catch, excitedly shouting to their fellow fishermen. Yet, what mind-stretching questions must have been racing through their heads! How had Jesus, from off on the shore, known where the fish were? Was it a miracle? It must have been! But how? Why?

As they pulled the wiggly, flopping fish into the boat, the words Jesus had spoken to Peter long ago suddenly echoed in his mind: "Follow me, and I will make you fishers of men."[1]

During His life on earth our Master gave us a plan for successful fishing . . . a model for making disciples. There is a vast potential catch available on 'the other side of the boat,' if we follow His plan. It is a way that can result in many new people coming into a life-changing relationship with Christ and His church. A plan that results in a new spiritual dimension in our own lives . . . new effectiveness in making disciples . . . new ministry and growth for our churches in fulfilling His command to "Go and make disciples."

The Master's Plan—God's Purpose

"For God so loved the world, that He gave His only Son, that whoever believes in Him should not perish, but have eternal life. For God did not send His Son into the world to judge the world; but that the world should be saved through Him."[2]

But how could the world that God so loved ever hear and believe such an awesome act of love? Jesus, in a conversation with His Father, supplies the answer: "I have sent them to the world, just as you sent Me to the world . . . that the world may believe that you did send me."[3] The Lord made His disciples' task crystal clear: "You shall be My witnesses both in Jerusalem, and in all Judea and Samaria, and even to the remotest parts of the earth."[4]

What were they to "witness" about? Again, Christ was specific and direct: "Thus it is written, that the Christ should suffer and rise again from the dead the third day; and that repentance for forgiveness of sins should be proclaimed in His name to all nations—beginning from Jerusalem. You are witnesses of these things."[5]

God, speaking to us through Scripture, presents a startlingly clear statement of His desire and unswerving purpose that lost mankind be reached and brought into His fellowship. Christ's birth, crucifixion, and resurrection were for the purpose of reconciling men and women with their Creator. Passage after passage in the Bible clearly underscores God's will "that all people be saved and come to a knowledge of the truth."[6]

The Master's Plan—The Commission

In a final summary of His earthly life and purpose, Christ turned over His own commission from God to His followers. As His Father had sent him, so he was sending them.[7] It was a life-encompassing challenge that could not be misinterpreted: "Go therefore and make disciples of all nations, baptizing them in the name of the Father and the Son and the Holy Spirit, teaching them to observe all that I commanded you . . ."[8]

This great commission to His followers, repeated on several occasions, reflects God's eternal purpose that all people everywhere have the opportunity to become disciples of Jesus Christ. It was this command of God through Jesus Christ that exerted singular direction on the early church. Central in all of Christ's teaching was the assumption that to follow Him meant to become participants in His mission.[9] When Christ gave the church its final directive, there was no question but that this command was to be given top priority. Christ did not accept the idea of a sideline disciple.

The expectation that all who received Jesus Christ as Lord and Savior would become His faithful and active disciples appears to have been widely held by first century Christians. What the apostle Paul affirmed they virtually assumed was true of themselves: "We are ambassadors for Christ, as though God were entreating multitudes through us, saying to them: We beg you on behalf of Christ, to be reconciled to God."[10]

Being His follower assumed not only an active

commitment to His Lordship, but also included active
involvement in the propogation of His Gospel. By definition,
disciples became "fishers of men." Christ's central desire for
His disciples was that, when He was gone, they would have
ingrained in their hearts and minds the conviction that the
Son of Man had come to seek and to save those who were
lost. His words, now called the Great Commission, were
simply a restatement of His entire life and teaching, as He
endeavored to make the matter as simple and easy to
understand as possible . . . "go and make disciples."[11]

The Master's Plan—Make Disciples

The words of Christ in Matthew 28:19-20 communicate
vividly Christ's understanding of a disciple. He saw a disciple
as one who becomes a follower, who is taught, who is
nurtured in the faith, who in turn goes out to make disciples,
who are then taught and nurtured in the faith, who then in
turn go out.

The perpetual multiplying of disciples reflects Christ's
strategy for reaching "the uttermost parts of the earth." This
strategy, as Luke records, became the basis of the explosive
growth of the early church: ". . . the number of disciples was
multiplied . . ." (Acts 6:1); ". . . and the number of disciples
multiplied in Jerusalem greatly . . ." (Acts 6:7); ". . . the
churches . . . upheld by the Holy Spirit, were multiplied" (Acts
9:31).

Christ expects every disciple to be a witness. Witnessing
to the Good News is simply the expression of Christian
discipleship. Acts 1:8 provides an important key to Christ's
expectations of His disciples. He said, "You shall be my
witnesses. . . ." The Greek verb in this command is actually in
the declarative form. Had Christ used the imperative verb "to
be," it would have implied a conscious activity or planned
action. Rather, Christ meant that *being* His witness was to be
a natural, assumed part of the disciple's life-style. This
natural, normal dimension of the disciple's life is God's secret
to fulfilling the Great Commission!

The Master's Plan—As Followed by the Early Church

The Gospel was shared so that people all around the world would have faith in Christ and obey Him.[12] And Luke records that people did respond in faith and obedience: "The word of God kept on spreading; the number of disciples continued to increase greatly in Jerusalem and a great many of the priests became obedient to the faith."[13]

What underlying principles caused those first-century Christians to achieve such remarkable success in making disciples?

Why were they described as "men who have turned the world upside-down?"[14]

1. The Goal Was Clear—Make Disciples. Being a disciple in the early church meant a first-hand involvement in the mission of Christ—making disciples. The goal was clear and all-encompassing.

An important facet of the early church's disciple-making goal was to continually expand this base of new disciples. In the book, *Back to Basics,* the authors note that "inherent in being saved was that the redeemed share the Good News. Being a Christian meant worshiping God; it meant doing good to all men, especially those of the household of faith. It meant expecting the Lord to return. It meant sins forgiven. *But above and beyond these, it meant telling people that the Savior had come*—that eternal life was theirs by believing in Him—that believing gave them the right to become children of God."[15]

A new convert's commitment to Christ included the assumption that he/she reproduce themselves and continue in the disciple-making chain. New disciples were instruments used by the Holy Spirit . . . in making disciples. Noted mission strategist George Peters observes that "the total program of indoctrination was designed to *make disciples* as they [the apostles] had been instructed by their Master to do. For the apostles, this meant to equip the believer for the ministry of their calling (Ephesians 4:11-16), and to qualify

A DISCIPLE IS . . .
A Ten-Minute Bible Study

The Lord's mandate to His Church rings loud and clear: "make disciples." What is a disciple? What is the process by which one becomes a disciple? What are characteristics of a disciple?

To begin to answer these questions, an introductory Bible study is helpful. Locate and read the following verses, then briefly answer the related question:

I. What is a disciple?

A disciple is a believer.
How does one become a believer? (John 11:25,26; Acts 16:30,31)

_____

_____

A disciple is a follower.
How does one become a follower? (Matthew 16:24; John 13:15)

_____

_____

A disciple is a learner.
What are the marks of a learner? (John 8:31,32; II Timothy 2:15)

_____

_____

THE MASTER'S PLAN—MAKING DISCIPLES

A disciple is a witness.
To what does he/she witness? (Mark 5:18,19;
I Peter 3:15)

_____

_____

A disciple is baptized.
How does baptism express a disciple's commitment?
(Acts 2:38,41,42; Acts 22:16)

_____

_____

A disciple is a reproducer.
What is a disciple to reproduce? (Matthew 28:19;
John 15:8)

_____

_____

II. List two characteristics of a disciple given in John 8:12 and 13:35.

1. _____

2. _____

III. Write your own definition of a present-day disciple.

_____

_____

them to give intelligent and reasonable answers for the hope
that was in them (I Peter 3:15)."[16]

2. Every Christian—A Witness. Inherent in the
definition of a "disciple" was one who shared the Good News
with others. For the early Christians, making disciples was
not seen as a compartmentalized activity, or the responsibility
assigned to a designated few. Rather, by its very nature, it was
an integral part of the lifestyle of every believer. In observing
the characteristics of the New Testament church, a noted
church historian has observed that "every member was
mobilized and actively involved . . . all functioned as
responsible members in the body life of the church."[17]

First-century Christians told the story of Christ simply and
graciously. Each believer's actions and attitudes confirmed
the centrality of Christ in life. Christians vouched for the way
the Lord had met all their needs. As Christians
enthusiastically exemplified how the realities of Christ were a
consistent part of everyday experiences, they presented a
convincing witness. Naturally and winsomely, these
Christians told of "the hope that was within them."

In the film THE GREAT COMMISSION SUNDAY
SCHOOL, Donald McGavran provides an insight into this
contagious spread of the Gospel: "Some of the greatest
growth of the church took place when refugee Christians
spread out across Judea. The Bible says, 'They preached the
Word.' Well, they didn't stand up in pulpits and preach. They
met people as they fled from Jerusalem and told them about
Jesus."[18]

Although fellowship with members of the Body was a vital
part of the believer's life, they did not remain in the "holy
huddle." Scripture records that everywhere they journeyed,
early Christians witnessed to the claims of Christ. While there
are only three references in the New Testament to those who
are "evangelists" (with the special gift of evangelism),
Scripture contains over 120 references to the broader
commission to all members of the Church to preach the

Gospel and make disciples.[19] The early Christians did not discount the command of making disciples simply because they lacked the gift of evangelist. Witnessing to their new faith was a lifestyle of every Christian and every Church. By naturally communicating their faith, they became God's instruments for bringing many people into His Kingdom.

3. Compassion—Permeating the Mission. The early Christians knew the deep concern their Lord had for "lost sheep." Jesus expressed His divine love even toward the unloved. He loved Matthew and Zacchaeus—despised tax collectors; He loved Roman centurions—the hated overlords of Judea; He loved lepers; He loved the blind, the lame, the halt. Christ's love for the multitudes, the children, the outcasts of society must have been told and retold by the first believers.

The early church mirrored their Master's compassion. Koinonia was one of the church's hallmarks: its members jointly participated in the life of Christ in their midst. The church was a loving, caring community. These first-century Christians expressed compassion in the daily routines of everyday living—the many garments Dorcas made and gave to the poor;[20] the sharing of property and possessions, as anyone might need.[21]

In writing to the Corinthians, Paul warmed with those often repeated and sometimes uncomprehended verses, "If I speak with the tongues of men and of angels, but do not have love, I have become a noisy gong or a clanging cymbal."[22] Compassion was a normal fruit of the Spirit. Compassion is one of the seeds of New Testament church growth.[23]

4. Relationships—The Means for Sharing the Master's Love. While the goal of the early Christian was, as Christ had commanded, to make disciples, there was a definite process by which the early church grew so explosively. The means of church growth was through the individual Christian's interlocking social system—the family, friends and associates. Christ often commanded new believers to return to their "households" (friends and family) and tell them of the Good News. Michael Green, in *Evangelism and the Early Church,* observes that the New Testament church religiously adhered to the strategy of using *"households"* in the Christian advance.[24] Luke records how those in the homes of Christians responded to the Gospel, with the result that "each day God added to them all who were being saved."[25]

Why were these households of friends and family so receptive to the Gospel? Two reasons: first, the caring and love which characterized the household relationships implied a level of trust, friendship and common concern. In the household, a person's concerns and convictions were respected and listened to. Second, those intimate with the new believer could witness the reality of a life changed by the power of the Master's love. Such a change in a person's lifestyle naturally had a significant impact on one's friends and family.

The early Christians knew that when the message of God's love was heard and demonstrated by those who were known and trusted, who were "their kind of people," the barriers of distrust and suspicion lowered and receptivity to the Good News increased tremendously. Thus the members of the early church continued Christ's example of making new disciples, as the Good News of God's love moved quickly and naturally along the lines of relationships.

5. Receptive People—The Point of Concentration.
Christ left no doubt concerning the importance of concentrating on receptive people. In the parable of the sower Jesus graphically illustrated the concept of receptivity as He explained that the seed sown on good soil is the man who both hears and understands the message. Such a person's life shows a good crop of thirty times, sixty, or a hundred times what was sown.[26] There seemed no doubt in

Christ's mind that the "seeds" should be planted in "fertile soil."

The Apostle Paul utilized the pattern of focusing his evangelistic activity on responsive people. He was so convinced of the importance of preaching Christ to people who were open that he asked the Colossians to pray ". . . that God may open up to us a door for the Word, so that we may speak forth the mystery of Christ."[27] In Corinth, God told Paul, "I have much people in this city." God wanted him to concentrate on the city of Corinth because there were many responsive people there.[28] In Ephesus, Paul writes, "But I will tarry at Ephesus, for a great door is open to me."[29]

Scripture also records the results of preaching to receptive people. "And when they [Paul and Barnabas] had arrived and gathered the church together, they began to report all things that God had done with them and how He had opened a door to the Gentiles."[30]

The disciple-making efforts of the early church were fruitful, and the church grew as a result of its members communicating the Gospel to clearly receptive segments of the population—whom God had prepared!

6. The Mission—Directed and Empowered by the Holy Spirit. These Christians knew their source of strength—the Holy Spirit who empowered them to live up to the high calling left by Christ Jesus. The Holy Spirit is revealed as the great strategist throughout Acts. He is indisputably the Superintendent of the great missionary endeavor. He empowers and initiates, guides and directs. George Peters observes that "As the goal of the church seen in Acts 1:8 gradually unfolded, the Holy Spirit surely motivated the church in its onward movement. On the day of Pentecost believers received the baptism of the Holy Spirit."[31]

Evidence of this direct effusion and guidance of the Spirit abounds in the Acts of the Apostles. One recalls how Philip, after having been significantly used by the Spirit to bring many Samaritans to Christ, was guided to reach an

Ethiopian eunuch with the Gospel.[32]

And the beginnings of the evangelization of the Gentiles was likewise under the Spirit's direction: "While Peter was reflecting on the vision, the Spirit said to him, 'Behold, three men are looking for you. But arise, go downstairs and accompany them without misgivings, for I have sent them Myself.' "[33]

The Holy Spirit continued as an active part of the spread of the Gospel: "And while they were ministering to the Lord and fasting, the Holy Spirit said, 'Set apart for Me Barnabas and Saul for the work to which I have called them.' "[34]

The pages of the New Testament tell again and again of men and women who, through faith in Jesus Christ, were given access through the Spirit to the Father. Filled with unshakable certainty that God had, through Christ, opened the way of salvation, they multiplied churches throughout the land.[35]

The Holy Spirit not only directed the mission of the early church, He also empowered these believers to accomplish their Christ-ordained mission. The Lord Jesus specifically told them to wait for the Holy Spirit because He would give them power to be witnesses in Jerusalem, Judea, Samaria, and the uttermost parts of the world. [36] The Holy Spirit provided the power to fulfill the mandate which Christ had committed to them: "And with great power the apostles were giving witness to the resurrection of the Lord Jesus, and abundant grace was upon them all."[37]

7. Boldness—In the Extension of the Faith. In the forum in Rome, in Ephesus, in Lystra, the Scriptures do not portray Paul possessed with the spirit of compromise or timidity.[38] Instead, we read of the courageous yet loving proclamations made here and there by an ambassador of the one true God. Paul preached his message fearlessly, even though he was frequently mobbed, beaten, and ridiculed.

Boldness was no more a natural or inherent trait of the early Christians than it is today. The apostles needed to pray often to God asking for "boldness in preaching."[39]

"And when they had prayed, the place where they had gathered together was shaken, and they were all filled with the Holy Spirit, and began to speak the word of God with boldness."[40] The early believers did not shrink from trial or hardship. In its face they prayed for boldness. And Scripture testified to the fruits of this intense desire to communicate the Good News, no matter what the cost. "Now when they saw the boldness of Peter and John, and perceived that they were unlearned and ignorant, they marvelled."[41]

8. The Scriptures—A Reference Point. Concerning the New Testament church's use of the Scriptures, noted scholar Michael Green observes, "As these first-century Christians preached the Good News, one phrase 'the Word' seems to be the heart of what they communicated. Wherever they went these early believers spread the Word. So much so that when Luke means us to understand that the church expands, he tells us that the Word grew. The Word means, of course, their proclamation of Jesus on the basis of the Old Testament."[42]

The apostles, grounded in the Old Testament Scriptures, knew their Jewish audience regarded the Scriptures as absolute truth. "For it is written" held the potential for convincing even the Jewish skeptics. Again and again these disciple-makers pointed to Christ's birth, life, death, resurrection, and ascension as the fulfillment of the Old Testament prophecy; that God's eternal promise to reconcile mankind to Himself had at last been fulfilled.[43]

In dealing with those of Jewish background, early Christians made frequent use of verses or passages from Scripture. It is clear, from their quotation of the Old Testament, that they had a strong preference for particular passages—Psalms 110 was the most favored of all. They immersed themselves in the Word which they proclaimed. They gave themselves to studying and thinking out how they would proclaim this "Word."

The early Christians knew that God, who had spoken partially through the Old Testament Scriptures, had now spoken fully and completely through Jesus Christ. So the believers searched the Old Testament Scriptures for insights concerning the Messiah.

9. The Church—A Body of Believers. The New Testament frequently pictures the disciple of Christ in a group setting; a sheep in a flock, a soldier in the army, a limb in the body, a stone in a building.[44] Becoming a member of the early church was a shared corporate experience. "They worshiped together regularly at the Temple each day, met in small groups in homes for Communion, and shared their meals with great joy and thankfulness, praising God."[45]

The early church recognized that by meeting together the Body derived strength, encouragement, stimulation, and knowledge. "Let us hold fast the confession of our hope without wavering, for He who promised is faithful . . . not forsaking our own assembling together, as is the habit of some, but encouraging one another; and all the more as you see the day drawing near."[46]

For those first-century believers, there were no "See you next week" farewells, or the expectation for any member to "go it alone." The growing number of disciples gave personal attention to the needs of each other in the context of everyday living. No one was forgotten. Their faith had given them a mandate to love one another. Now they were putting it into action!

▶◀▶◀▶◀▶◀▶◀

The television was blaring as Diane opened the front door. In front of the set Chuck was sleeping soundly. Diane turned off the television which brought Chuck out of his sleep.

"Diane, you just got home?"

"Just walked in the door," answered Diane. "Sweetheart, you really missed a good meeting."

Chuck sat up, took off his glasses and tried rubbing the sleep out of his eyes.

"And what new evangelism techniques did you learn?"

"Chuck, it wasn't like that."

"Oh, come on, Diane, admit it. You learned three new methods for buttonholing people for Jesus. In fact your purse is probably packed with new 'miracle tracts' guaranteed to make people instant Christians."

Diane was exasperated. "Chuck, believe me. We didn't even talk about methods of witnessing. What we studied about was the early church and their strategy for disciple-making."

Chuck stood up. "Diane, can't you see what Pastor Austin's doing? He's setting you up. And next week you will learn what evangelism methods were used by the early church—and how we can use them today. Right?"

"You're probably right. But maybe we should learn to use their methods. After all, didn't they turn their world upside down?" Diane gave Chuck a parting smile and headed for the bedroom.

"But, Diane . . ."

It was too late. She was gone and the discussion was over.

Footnotes

1. Matthew 4:19
2. See John 3:16,17
3. John 17:18,21
4. Acts 1:8
5. Luke 24:46-48
6. See I Timothy 2:4
7. John 20:21
8. Matthew 28:19,20
9. Kenneth Van Wyk, "Educate for Church Growth," CHURCH GROWTH: AMERICA, March/April 1978, p. 7.
10. II Corinthians 5:20
11. Matthew 28:19
12. Romans 16:26
13. See Acts 6:7
14. Acts 17:6
15. Donald McGavran and Win Arn, Back to Basics in Church Growth, (Wheaton: Tyndale, 1981), pp. 108,109.

32   **THE MASTER'S PLAN**

16. George W. Peters, *A Theology of Church Growth* (Grand Rapids: Zondervan, 1981), p. 190.
17. George W. Peters, op. cit., p. 218.
18. Win Arn Productions, THE GREAT COMMISSION SUNDAY SCHOOL (Pasadena: Christian Communication), color, 28-minute film, 1981.
19. Robert E. Coleman, *The Mind of the Master* (Old Tappan: Fleming H. Revell Co., 1977), p. 9.
20. See Acts 9:39
21. See Acts 2:45
22. I Corinthians 13:1
23. Donald McGavran and Win Arn, op. cit., p. 79.
24. Michael Green, *Evangelism in the Early Church* (Grand Rapids: Eerdmans, 1970), p. 210.
25. Acts 2:47
26. Matthew 13:23
27. Colossians 4:3
28. Acts 18:8-11
29. I Corinthians 16:8,9
30. Acts 14:27
31. George W. Peters, op.cit., pp. 223,219.
32. Acts 8:29
33. Acts 10:19-20
34. Acts 13:2
35. Donald McGavran and Win Arn, op.cit., pp. 91,92.
36. Ibid., p. 106.
37. Acts 4:33
38. See Ephesians 6:19
39. See Acts 4:29
40. Acts 4:31
41. Acts 4:13
42. Michael Green, op.cit., pp. 35,36.
43. See Acts 13:32-35
44. Green, op.cit., p. 54.
45. Acts 2:46
46. Hebrews 10:23,25

How New Disciples Are Made

THE *OIKOS* FACTOR

"**J**oshua, a Jewish merchant from Rome, walked briskly along the cobble-stone road. He knew, as he passed more and more people, that he was getting closer. He had heard much and thought often about the city of David; a thought shared by every Jew throughout the Roman world. Forty years earlier Herod the Great had begun a major restoring project in Jerusalem to return it to its former grandeur. Not since the time of King Solomon had such palaces, citidels, amphitheaters, viaducts, and public monuments been built. So magnificent were these buildings Herod had begun that some were still being completed. Joshua had heard that visitors were overwhelmed by the city's splendor."

Chuck restlessly changed position. Pastor Austin was doing another of his fictional, quasi-biblical narratives and Chuck wasn't interested.

"The winding road made its way over a hill of gnarled olive trees. Joshua's pulse quickened . . . his pace increased. As a Jewish merchant, he had 'officially' made this trip for business reasons. But secretly Joshua had always longed for a reason to take the several-week journey from Rome to Jerusalem and see the city of his dreams. Nearing the top of

Pastor Austin was doing another of his fictional, quasi-biblical narratives. . . .

the last hill, he no longer noticed or nodded to travelers passing on the road. He was sure that on the other side of the hill . . . He broke into a run, sandals clapping against the cobblestones.

"Then, he saw it. He gazed transfixed. Joshua could not believe he was actually there. Across the valley, set among the surrounding hills, was Jerusalem . . . 'the perfection of beauty' in the words of Lamentations, 'the joy of all the world.' "

Why, Chuck wondered, had he let Diane talk him into coming to Session 2 of Pastor Austin's seminar on "Disciple-making . . . The Master's Plan"? Was it because Diane had been so insistent? Or was it because, as a committed Christian, he carried guilt feelings about his lack of fruitfulness as a witness for his Lord?

"As Joshua approached the city, he could see how the massive stone wall which surrounded it had been damaged, repaired, and enlarged over the centuries. At intervals along

the wall were located massive gateways where people
streamed in and out of the city. Just inside each gate was a
customs station where publicans collected taxes on all goods
entering and leaving the city. Joshua explained his mission
to the gatekeeper, and was told to report to the customs
center near the temple where an officer would explain the
regulations.

"Once inside the city, Joshua faced a bewildering maze of
dusty winding streets and alleyways. As he pushed his way
through the crowds, slowly making his way toward the
temple, his senses were assaulted by the sounds of voices
raised in bartering or in song, the braying of donkeys, odors
of cooking bread, bleating of sheep soon to be sacrificed. In
the excitement, Joshua nearly forgot to ask directions to his
brother-in-law Benjamin's house where he would be staying
while in Jerusalem."

Chuck glanced at Diane. She was far away . . . with
Pastor Austin in first-century Jerusalem. Chuck discreetly
checked his watch. When would Pastor Austin get to his
point? Who cares about some imaginary Jewish merchant
from the first century?

"The next day Joshua spent as a tourist walking through
the city. Since it was the holiday feast of Pentecost, most
merchants were not doing business. As Joshua entered the
marketplace, he noticed a gathering on the far side of the
court. It seemed to be a political meeting or a public debate.

"Walking closer, Joshua saw a large, bearded man
standing above the others, speaking to the crowd. Suddenly
Joshua's heart jumped. He couldn't believe what he was
hearing. The Jewish man was speaking in perfect and fluent
Latin, a language Joshua had not heard since he left the
Roman ship on the coast of Israel. He listened.

"The man speaking called himself Peter, and spoke of
strange but fascinating things. Peter spoke of the Messiah,
foretold by the prophets, and that this Messiah had already
come. In fact, Peter claimed that he had actually been with
the Messiah only days before! Peter's message filled Joshua

Why, Chuck wondered, had he let Diane talk him into coming to this disciple-making class?

with a strange sense of intrigue. It was unthinkable that the Messiah had actually come. Everyone would know! Yet the story this man told sounded reasonable and compelling. Could the long awaited Messiah actually have come?

"Later that day Joshua responded to Peter's message about the risen Christ and His love. Joshua and 3000 others were baptized. He hurried home to tell Benjamin, his brother-in-law, and his family of this exciting new dimension to the Jewish faith. That night as Joshua, overflowing with joy, shared the events of the day, Benjamin, Benjamin's wife Miriam, and their whole family made the decision to follow Jesus, the Messiah.

"In order to learn more about his new faith, Joshua stayed in Jerusalem longer than he originally planned. He, Benjamin, and Miriam joined the other believers as they devoted themselves 'to the apostles teaching and to fellowship, to the breaking of bread and to prayer.'

"Joshua wrote home to his wife Ruth and the children to

explain his delay. He told them of his new faith, and sent the letter by Ananiah, a friend in Rome who was visiting Jerusalem and who also became a disciple at Pentecost.

"By the time Joshua himself returned to Rome, his family had already become disciples of Jesus the Messiah. Between Joshua's letter and Ananiah's personal testimony, they couldn't resist this faith that fulfilled and completed their Jewish beliefs. Joshua began sharing the apostles' teaching with his family and with Ananiah. Soon Ananiah's family and servants also came to the Lord.

"Meanwhile, Joshua returned to his import-export business. He gathered his employees around to tell them of this new faith. Many of them believed and asked Joshua to help them share the Good News with their families.

"Whether he knew it or not, Joshua was part of a process of making disciples that would be the way the Christian movement would eventually become the most widespread faith and force on earth. And a key element in that process was the communication of God's love through an established network of social relationships which the Greek New Testament calls 'oikos'."

Almost imperceptibly Chuck shook his head. Doesn't Pastor Austin realize that we don't live in the first century? What may have worked then doesn't necessarily work today!

◄►◄►◄►◄►◄

Chuck's questions of the applicability of 2,000 year old principles deserves an answer. But first let's examine the meaning of the new word *"oikos"* introduced by Pastor Austin.

The word *oikos* is the Greek word for "household". In the Graeco-Roman culture *oikos* described not only the immediate family in the house, but included servants, servants' families, friends, and even business associates. "An oikos was one's sphere of influence, his/her social system composed of those related to each other through common kinship ties, tasks, and territory."[2]

The Household and the Old Testament

The Old Testament pictures the household ("*bayit*" in the Hebrew) as including several generations in a family. In the book *Anthology of the Old Testament,* Hans Walter Wolff observes that "A household usually contained four generations, including men, married women, unmarried daughters, slaves of both sexes, persons without citizenship, and 'sojourners,' or resident foreign workers."[3] Old Testament Scripture confirms again and again the significance and uniqueness of the household and the family. God's original promise to Abraham included the provision that through him ". . . all families of the earth shall be blessed."[4] "The word 'families,'" according to noted biblical historian Cornell Goerner, "does not refer to the simple family unit, composed of a man, his wife, and their children, but rather describes the extended families, or the *oikos.*"[5]

Later God directed His people: ". . . in the presence of the Lord your God, you and your families *(bayit)* shall rejoice in everything you have put your hand to, because the Lord your God has blessed you."[6]

There are many other references to the centrality of the family and household in the lives of God's people: "And therefore rejoice before the Lord your God; you, your sons and daughters, your menservants and maidservants, and the Levites from your towns. . . ."[7]

"Then you and your household shall eat there in the presence of the Lord your God and rejoice."[8] ". . . and the family which the Lord shall take shall come by households. . . ."[9]

Oikos and the New Testament

God continues to focus on the household (friends, extended family, associates) in the New Testament in His plans for communicating to mankind. The Gospels, Acts, and Epistles show that the bridges of *oikos* were used regularly as a means to spread the Good News. After healing a demon possessed man, Jesus told him, "Go home to your friends (*oikos*) and tell them what wonderful thing God has done for you; and how merciful He has been."[10]

After Zacchaeus was converted, Jesus said to him, "Today salvation has come to this house *(oikos)*."[11]

When Jesus healed the son of a royal official, "he and all his household *(oikos)* believed."[12]

Levi followed Jesus, and invited his fellow tax collectors— his *"oikos"*—to come to dinner, and as a result many followed Christ.[13]

The Apostle Peter came to Christ as a result of someone in his *oikos:* "The first thing Andrew did was to find his brother Simon and tell him, 'We have found the Messiah.' "[14] And another disciple, Nathaniel, came to Christ as a result of his friend Philip who "went to find Nathaniel and told him 'we have met the man spoken of by Moses in the Law. . . .' "[15]

Following Christ's resurrection and ascension, it was this same pattern of the Gospel moving through the *oikos* which caused the early church to explode. Noted church historian Kenneth Scott Latourette has observed that, "the primary change agents in the spread of faith . . . were the men and women who earned their livelihood in some purely secular manner, and spoke of their faith to those whom they met in this natural fashion."[16]

In the book of Acts, chapter 10, the story is recorded of the first non-Jewish household to respond to the message of the apostles. It took a special vision from God to convince Peter that it was all right to tell Gentiles about Christ. But when the invitation came from the centurion Cornelius, Peter was ready. When he and several other believers arrived, they found Cornelius "had called together his relatives and close friends"[17]—his *oikos.* When Peter finished sharing the Gospel, Scripture records that the entire household responded.[18] Later, as Peter tried to convince the Jewish Christians in Jerusalem that the Gospel could also be for the Gentiles, he told of a vision from God and a call from Caesarea where he went and spoke, and an entire household was saved.[19]

In another example, Paul and his companions shared
Christ with a business woman named Lydia, outside the city
of Philippi. The Bible records that she responded to their
message and that she and the members of her household
were baptized.[20]

Shortly thereafter, Paul and Silas were thrown into jail. As
they were praying and singing hymns, an earthquake freed
all the prisoners of their chains. Rather than face death
because of the escaped prisoners, the jailer prepared to kill
himself. But Paul assured him they were still there and the
jailer asked, "Men, what must I do to be saved?" They replied,
"Believe in the Lord Jesus, and you will be saved, you and
your household." "Then they spoke the word of the Lord to
him and to all the others in his house (oikos) . . . The jailer
and all his family were baptized, and the whole family was
filled with joy, because the had come to believe in God."[21]

Church growth authority Donald McGavran observes that
believers in the early churches had relatives and friends
scattered across the Roman Empire. "According to the
record, some of the Christians who had first spoken of the
faith to Greeks in Antioch came from Cyprus. They probably
belonged to families who had connections on both the island
and the mainland. Having won their relatives in Antioch, it
was natural for them to think of winning their unconverted
relatives, Jews and Greeks, in Cyprus."[22] Even as the new
Christians were thinking of their relatives, the Holy Spirit was
preparing Barnabas and Saul for a missionary trip which
would begin in Cyprus. As the Antioch congregation
discussed the Lord's leading and made arrangements for the
trip, people with relatives along the proposed route would
surely have made suggestions. In the book *Bridges of God,*
McGavran recreates the scene:

"Some Jewish woman in Antioch may have said to Paul: 'I
have a brother in Iconium. He has, for many years, longed for
the coming of the Messiah. How I wish it were possible for
him to hear you! He has a large house and has prospered in

business. He would give you a genuine welcome. Do let me send him word.'

"Wherever he went, Paul must have had someone's brother-in-law or second cousin or aunt or uncle to look up. He could approach such a person with a message: 'Simon sends his greetings, and says to tell you the family is well. He hopes you and your household are well, and he said that you might like to hear the message we bear, that the Messiah has come and brought a new way of life.' Think of the great receptivity such contacts would have produced! It is, to us, an inescapable inference that Paul at Antioch must have known of many such relatives and must have realized their enormous importance in the extension of the faith."[23]

Paul was not the only one spreading the Gospel. Thousands of Christians were telling friends and relatives in their *oikos* about Jesus. In the film BUT . . . I'M JUST A LAYMAN, the observation is made: "You probably think the phenomenal growth of the early church took place because of a few dedicated apostles. Absolutely not! It grew explosively because of the laity—ordinary men and women telling their friends and family about Jesus Christ and the Good News of salvation."[24]

Michael Green observes that "The early Christians knew that when the message of faith was heard and demonstrated by friends and family who were known and trusted . . . receptivity to the Gospel increased tremendously."[25]

Chuck could wait no longer. He raised his hand. "But, Pastor, what basis do we have for assuming that this 'oikos' concept works today?"

Diane was a little embarrassed by Chuck's bluntness, but Pastor Austin didn't seem to mind the question. "Good question, Chuck. I think the best way to answer that would be to take a few minutes and share some of the various ways some of us have come to Christ and to

"But pastor, what basis do we have for assuming that this *oikos* concept works today?"

this church. Who'll be first?"

An older woman in the front row raised her hand. Standing, she told the group how she was now in the church because of a friend from church who lived in her mobile home park. This friend invited her to attend some meetings in the women's circle at the church. She came to the meetings and in time made a Christian commitment. Even though her friend had since passed away, she has continued as an active Christian and member of the church.

A younger woman, about 25, told how she had come to Christ through her Christian parents. When she moved to this town to take a job she began looking for a church. A friend of hers at work was attending this church and so it was a natural step into the church after she had visited a few times.

A middle-aged man then told how one of his cousins, who lived in town, had introduced him and the family to Christ and this church.

"Chuck, does that answer your question?"

"Yeah. I'd say that answers it." Chuck turned to Diane, who gave him an *"I told you so"* smile.

●◄●►◄●►◄●►►

The Importance of *Oikos* Today

Webs of *common kinship* (the larger family), *common friendship* (friends and neighbors) and *common associates* (special interests, work relationships, and recreation) are still the paths most people follow in becoming Christians today.

Research conducted by the Institute of American Church Growth of Pasadena, California, on why people have come to Christ and the Church, provides astonishing support on the *oikos* process at work today.[26] Over 14,000 lay people have been asked the question: "What or who was responsible for your coming to Christ and your church?" One of the following eight responses was usually given: (1) some said a *'special need'* brought them to Christ and the church; (2) some responded they just *'walked in'*; (3) others listed the *'pastor'*; (4) some indicated *'visitation'*; (5) others mentioned the *'Sunday School'*; (6) a few listed *'evangelistic crusade* or *television program'*; (7) others recalled that the church *'program'* attracted them; (8) finally, some people responded *'friend/relative'* as being the reason they are now in Christ and the church.

What percentage of people came to their new relationship with Christ and their church through each category? Here are the results:

Special need	1-2%
Walk-In	2-3%
Pastor	5-6%
Visitation	1-2%
Sunday School	4-5%
Evangelistic Crusade . . .	½ of 1%
Church Program	2-3%
Friend/Relative	75-90%

The conclusion is clear: the great majority of people today can trace their "spiritual roots" directly to a friend or a relative as the major reason they are in Christ and their church. (Do some research in your own church to see if this holds true.)

Here are some actual examples of how people come to Christ and the church today. The Prince of Peace Lutheran Church in Carrollton, Texas, where Dr. Steve Wagner is pastor, is typical . . .

Two members of the church, husband and wife, invited a non-Christian neighbor couple to their church's family enrichment program. The couple enjoyed a pleasurable and positive experience. Later the husband and wife invited these non-Christian friends to a Sunday morning worship service, and the couple continued to attend together. Soon the wife made a commitment to Christ. She enrolled their four-year-old boy in the church pre-school program. A few months later, her husband came to Christ and they both joined the church. Following their commitment, the new Christian mother encouraged a friend of hers to enroll her four-year-old in the church's pre-school program. And at the next family enrichment program, the new Christian couple brought a non-Christian friend and the wife's brother. The brother began attending a Sunday morning worship, enrolled in a church membership class, and has since become a Christian. He, in turn, is presently sharing his faith with his parents.

This natural web of relationships, in a short period of time, has resulted in eight new people making professions of faith and becoming responsible church members. And the web is just beginning.

Another example: A sales manager and member of Ness Avenue Baptist Church in Winnipeg, reached two members of his *oikos* (two work associates) for Christ and the church. The pastor of the church has identified thirty-four people that have come to Christ from this web of *oikos* members.

In the Grove City, Ohio, Nazarene Church there is a

program built around *oikos* called "The Family Tree." It began as a result of a young couple coming to Christ and the church, who have since been responsible (either directly or indirectly) for bringing thirty-five other adults (plus thirty-two children) to Christ and the church.

Pages 46-49, reprinted from the book *Growth: A New Vision for the Sunday School,* visually illustrate the *oikos* phenomena as traced in a Free Methodist Church in Bellingham, Washington.[27] It started with a young man named Ron Johnson. Look at the relationships over which the Gospel traveled. (Names, ages, and the dates they became Christian are all given.)

The centuries-old concept of *oikos,* or webs, continues to be the bridge over which the Good News of God's love travels naturally.

Why *Oikos* Is Effective

Why do people respond so positively to the Gospel as it travels through these "webs" of relationships?

1. **Oikos Relationships Provide a Natural Network for Sharing the Good News of God's Redemptive Love.** The new Christian, who has discovered the genuine joy of experiencing God's grace, is naturally eager to tell others. He wants those closest to him to share in this new freedom and joy. The *oikos* of friends, relatives, and associates is the most natural place for a new Christian to share this new found joy with people . . . people who mean the most to him.

"I believe Nancy and Susan are good examples of how the 'oikos' principle has worked in our church," Pastor Austin smiled at two young women in the second row. "Susan, would you mind sharing with the group how you and Nancy became disciples?"

"Sure," said Susan. "Nancy and I had been roommates for a little over a year. We got along well together, and enjoyed each other's company. Neither one of us were Christians, and

RON JOHNSON
28 yrs., 5/74

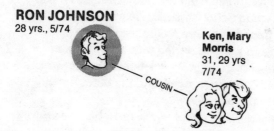

**Ken, Mary
Morris**
31, 29 yrs
7/74

COUSIN

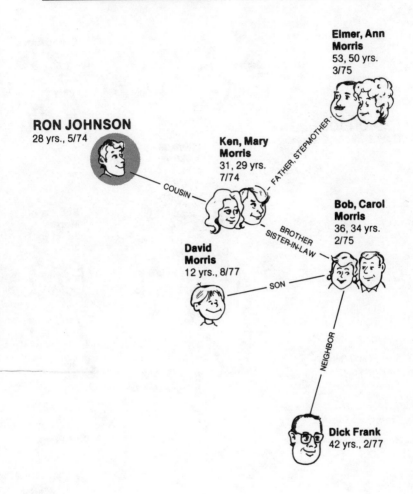

Elmer, Ann Morris
53, 50 yrs.
3/75

RON JOHNSON
28 yrs., 5/74

Ken, Mary Morris
31, 29 yrs.
7/74

COUSIN

FATHER, STEPMOTHER

Bob, Carol Morris
36, 34 yrs.
2/75

BROTHER
SISTER-IN-LAW

David Morris
12 yrs., 8/77

SON

NEIGHBOR

Dick Frank
42 yrs., 2/77

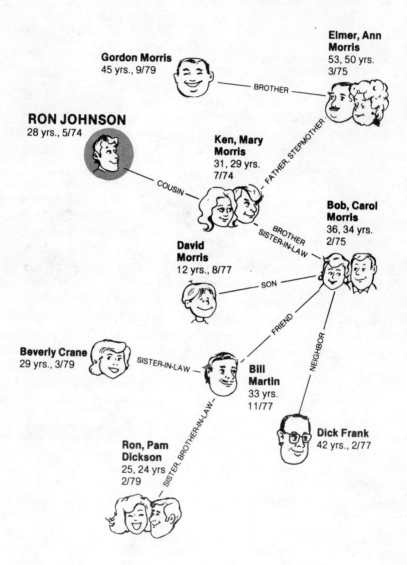

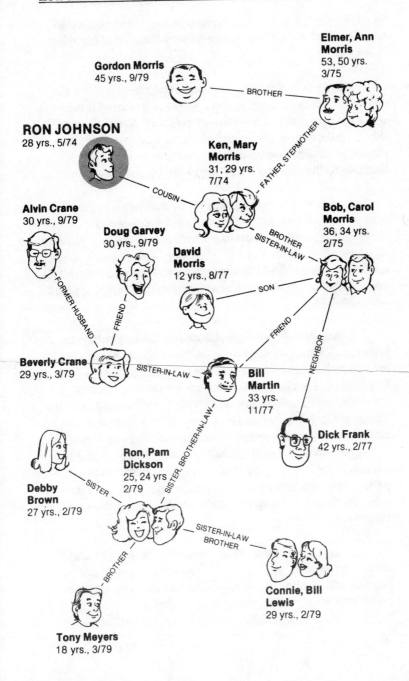

Elmer, Ann Morris
53, 50 yrs.
3/75

Gordon Morris
45 yrs., 9/79

— BROTHER —

RON JOHNSON
28 yrs., 5/74

Ken, Mary Morris
31, 29 yrs.
7/74

COUSIN

FATHER, STEPMOTHER

Bob, Carol Morris
36, 34 yrs.
2/75

Alvin Crane
30 yrs., 9/79

Doug Garvey
30 yrs., 9/79

David Morris
12 yrs., 8/77

BROTHER SISTER-IN-LAW

SON

FORMER HUSBAND

FRIEND

FRIEND

NEIGHBOR

Beverly Crane
29 yrs., 3/79

— SISTER-IN-LAW —

Bill Martin
33 yrs.
11/77

Dick Frank
42 yrs., 2/77

Debby Brown
27 yrs., 2/79

SISTER

Ron, Pam Dickson
25, 24 yrs
2/79

SISTER, BROTHER-IN-LAW

SISTER-IN-LAW
BROTHER

Connie, Bill Lewis
29 yrs., 2/79

BROTHER

Tony Meyers
18 yrs., 3/79

so it came as quite a shock to me one day when she came home and started talking about having committed her life to Jesus Christ."

2. **Oikos Members Are Receptive.** There is quite a difference between hearing the witness of a trusted friend, and hearing a "religious presentation" from a total stranger. When God's love is discussed with an *oikos* member, that person is usually open and receptive since he or she is listening to the experience of someone they know and trust.

"I remember," continued Susan, "when Nancy began explaining her new attitudes and belief, I was really interested. She still seemed to be normal; I mean, she hadn't all of a sudden freaked out or anything." Susan laughed and looked at Nancy. "And talking with her in our apartment, I felt comfortable asking questions and discussing her new ideas and faith."

3. **Oikos Relationships Allow for Unhurried and Natural Sharing of God's Love.** Relationships with *oikos* members, by their very nature, are regular and natural. Whether on a social outing or in the comfort of a living room, the relationships are usually easy and relaxed. And the Christian lifestyle demonstrates Christ's love in a variety of places, times, and situations. Communicating the Gospel is not squeezed into one short visit or presentation. Being a witness to the life-changing effects of God's love over a period of weeks, months, and even years, allows the *oikos* member time for thoughtful consideration about becoming a disciple.

"Although I was interested, I needed time to think about what it all meant," said Susan. "I had a lot of preconceived notions about what a Christian was and did, and I needed some time to see what Nancy's new commitment really meant to her. As days and months went by I saw some

significant changes in Nancy, and being around her and seeing what her faith meant to her had an important effect on my own thinking."

4. Oikos Relationships Provide Natural Support When the Web Member Comes to Christ.
When a friend or relative comes to faith, there is a natural source for nurture and encouragement. Since at least one Christian—the original web member—is close to the new convert and eager to see growth in his/her new life, new Christians are not left alone. There is someone to love, care for, and nurture them.

"After three months, I began attending some church events with Nancy," Susan recalled. "Six months later I decided to commit my life to Christ. As a young Christian it has meant a great deal to have Nancy's loving support helping me grow as a disciple."

5. Oikos Relationships Result in the Effective Assimilation of New Converts into the Church.
It is natural for the new Christian to begin attending church where his/her friend or family member belongs. Because of this "bridge," the new Christian can much more easily become associated with other Christians in a Sunday School class or fellowship group, and begin to build relationships and new friends within the Body.

"I really feel at home in this church, although at first it was 'Nancy's church.' But soon it became my church, too. I joined the Sunday School class where Nancy was a member, and met many new friends. The social activities sponsored by the church also helped me feel part of the group."

6. Oikos Relationships Tend to Win Entire Families.
When one or two people in a family come to Christ and the church, it is often the beginning of a process that results in the entire family becoming new disciples. As the entire family

grows together in Christ, the family unit is strengthened. On the other hand, if the entire family is not reached, conflict and fragmentation often result. Christians and non-Christians have different goals and priorities. Spiritual growth is more difficult and the new Christian may drop out of an active Christian life due to this lack of family support. An immediate emphasis should be placed on identifying and reaching others in a family, once one member has made a Christian commitment.

"After I made a commitment to Christ and joined this church," Susan concluded, "I immediately told my mother, brother, and sister-in-law of the exciting new discovery I had made. I'm hoping they, too, will soon discover the joy of being a Christian. Anyway, I'm praying for them."

7. **Oikos Relationships Provide a Constantly Enlarging Source of New Contacts.** Each new person reached for Christ and the church has his/her own group of relatives, friends and associates who are candidates for the Good News. Research shows that, on the average, each new Christian has twelve people in his/her *oikos* who are non-Christian. (Older Christians often have less; the average in most churches is about eight.) In most cases everyone in that new Christian's web is outside of Christ and a local church. The process of identifying receptive people and reaching out is never completed, because with each new Christian there are new contacts and opportunities.

Throughout the 2,000 year history of the church, God has richly blessed its growth through webs of *oikos* relationships.[28] The *oikos* concept is timely, yet timeless. It is planned, yet not contrived. It is founded on solid church growth research, experience, and principles found throughout Scripture. It is the way churches have grown, and continue to grow, as each new *oikos* member who comes to Christ and the church has his/her own web of friends and

"Wouldn't the Gospel have spread faster if the early church had had modern media," Chuck wondered aloud.

relatives, and the pattern continues.

◆<◆<◆<◆<◆<◆<

After the session Chuck cornered Pastor Austin with another question. "Wouldn't the gospel have spread faster," Chuck asked, "if the early church had been able to use modern media—like radio and television?"

Pastor Austin smiled and shook his head. "No, Chuck, I don't think so. The first century church had a better medium for communicating God's love."

"And what was that?"

"Well, it was what we talked about tonight . . . the oikos network. And, Chuck, it's still the best medium."

Footnotes

1. Acts 2:42
2. Ralph W. Neighbors, Jr., *Future Church* (Nashville: Broadman Press, 1980), p. 163.
3. Hans Walter Wolff, *Anthology of the Old Testament* (Philadelphia: Fortress Press, 1974), p. 215.

4. Genesis 12:3
5. Cornell Goerner, *All Nations in God's Purpose* (Nashville: Broadman Press, 1979), p. 23.
6. Deuteronomy 12:7
7. Deuteronomy 12:12
8. See Deuteronomy 14:26
9. Joshua 7:14
10. Mark 5:19
11. Luke 19:9
12. John 4:53
13. See Mark 2:14,15
14. John 1:41
15. John 1:45
16. Kenneth Scott Latourette, *A History of the Expansion of Christianity, Volume I: The First Five Centuries,* (New York: Harper, 1937), p. 116.
17. Acts 10:24
18. See Acts 10:44
19. See Acts 10 and 11
20. See Acts 16:15
21. Acts 16:30-34
22. Donald A. McGavran, *The Bridges of God* (New York: Friendship Press, 1968), p. 27.
23. Ibid., pp. 27-28.
24. Win Arn Productions, BUT . . . I'M JUST A LAYMAN (Pasadena: Christian Communication), color, 25-minute film, 1979.
25. Michael Green, *Evangelism in the Early Church* (Grand Rapids: Eerdmans, 1970), p. 210.
26. Charles Arn, Donald McGavran, Win Arn, *Growth: A New Vision for the Sunday School* (Pasadena: Church Growth Press, 1980), pp. 75,76.
27. Ibid., pp. 78-78C.
28. Donald A. McGavran, *Understanding Church Growth* (Grand Rapids: Eerdmans, 1970), pp. 359-363.

Key Principles of Disciple-Making

The bright morning sun had little effect on Chuck as he sat sipping his breakfast coffee. He had slept badly, tossing and turning most of the night.

"What's wrong, sweetheart?" asked Diane.

"I just can't do it!"

"Can't do what?"

"Diane, I just don't think I can share my faith. And I know that I should! I lay awake most of the night thinking about it."

"But, Chuck, why do you feel that way?"

"Well, that's what I've been wrestling with. I think it's because I feel inadequate. I mean, who am I to explain the Gospel to people? I've never even been to seminary!"

"But, Chuck, none of the Apostles ever went to seminary. And they did pretty well at sharing their faith!"

"Yeah, but they were apostles. Besides, I'm not good enough. You know I'm not, Diane."

"Chuck, stop putting yourself down. Did you ever think what would have happened if the first Christians had waited until they were perfect before sharing their faith? The church would have died right in the first century."

Chuck nodded. "I never thought of that. But, Diane, who would be interested in my witness?"

"What do you mean?"

"I just can't do it!"

"Well, you know how people are today. They're only interested in money . . . and things . . . and having a good time. No one's interested in the church . . . or my faith."

Diane placed her hand over his.

"Chuck, you believe that your relationship to Jesus Christ makes a difference in your life."

"Well, sure. I wouldn't be a Christian if I didn't. Diane, that's what bothers me most. I would like to share my faith . . . if I could!"

"God So Loved the World . . ."

God's unswerving purpose is the discipling of mankind. He calls His Church and each of His disciples to a deliberate commitment to see this happen. As we saw in the first chapter, this is the priority of Christ and the command to His Church.

Most Christians and churches believe this. The problem comes when church leaders and laity try to translate this "call to arms" into specific marching orders. "What can we as a church, or as individuals, really do that is significant? And how do we do it?" Indeed, this shortage of practical, "do-able" guidelines for effective church evangelism is one of the greatest frustrations in the church today. "Go and make disciples . . . fine, but how?"

It's for this reason that we are suggesting an important new approach to disciple-making in and through the local church. It is an approach and strategy that builds on new research in church growth previously unavailable to designers of evangelism programs. The new approach is not a program but a process . . . a process that builds on the natural "webs" of relationships which exist in every church. It is a process that can be a rewarding, fruitful experience for each participating church member. We call it *The Master's Plan!*

The Master's Plan is a unique merging of New Testament principles and modern church growth insights, designed to help you and your church more effectively respond to Christ's Great Commission where He has placed you.

The Master's Plan is a strategy of disciple-making to help lay church members identify and reach the people in their web, or *oikos,* for Christ and the Church. It is a process that works within natural characteristics of human behavior and relationships, and relates the unique needs of friends and relatives to Christ's work in their lives. *The Master's Plan* is a fulfilling, satisfying lifestyle for all church members. It is not an exercise in sweaty palms, stomach butterflies, or high degrees of anxiety, but is one of the most enjoyable experiences a Christian will have in his/her lifetime . . . guaranteed!

We are convinced that through the example of Christ and the early church, and through study of the church as it has grown throughout history and today, God has blessed the growth of His church when it has occurred through the households, and relationships, and webs of people. *The Master's Plan* builds on the scriptural insight that the

Christian message travels best over natural bridges of friendships and relationships (*oikos*). It is a disciple-making strategy that seeks to identify receptive people whom God has prepared, and win them while they are winnable.

The Master's Plan is based on the conviction that God wants His lost children found. The bottom line in effective evangelism is whether people are won to Christ and the church grows. The motivation behind a concern for effective disciple-making is the conviction that God desires His church to be effective in proclaiming the Gospel and making disciples. *The Master's Plan,* when incorporated and practiced in the local church, is an intentional and effective way to see this happen.

Principles of the Master's Plan

What are the cornerstones of this major, new approach to disciple-making in the local church? There are nine key principles in *The Master's Plan* disciple-making strategy. Here is a brief statement of each. (These principles are elaborated upon throughout the book.) As you consider this church growth model for disciple-making, examine these principles closely. Study them. Test them with your own experiences in evangelism and disciple-making. Question them. Use them.

Principle # 1   *Disciple-making is most effective when it is an intentional response by the local church to the Great Commission.*

In many churches today, the number of people, dollars, and time used for outreach forces one to conclude that in the natural course of church life, there is little intentionality evidenced for reaching people.

Intentionality in evangelism is the church's response to Christ's command to make disciples. It is an act of obedience, an acknowledgement of His Lordship. Intentionality in evangelism means that disciple-making becomes part of the priorities and goals of the church . . . part of its very reason for being. Intentionality in evangelism means the church regularly measures itself against the yardstick of the numbers of new disciples it produces. Intentionality in evangelism means that the church makes a commitment to disciple-making and sticks with it. It means that the purpose and activities of groups within the church include specific and intentional steps to bring new disciples into the local body of believers.

Such intentional evangelism does not automatically happen. In fact, a church often grows "inward" over time, becoming more concerned with its own survival and less concerned with its call to multiply itself.

But what does "intentional evangelism" mean? Is it a weekly calling program, or the employment of a minister of visitation, or a series of witness training meetings? Certainly some effort is better than none. Yet research indicates that in a typical church only 1 to 2 out of every 100 people came to their church as a result of a formal visitation program.[1] Intentionality in outreach means doing something. But it doesn't mean doing just anything. More than just good intentions are required. Effective evangelism requires insight and study as to what are the best and most productive intentional efforts that can be made. Some intentional efforts will be more effective in making disciples than others.

Effective disciple-making combines intentional growth principles with an "evangelistic mix" that fits the local church and its unique situation. Tremendous power results in a local church which intentionally focuses on specific growth goals. When staff, lay leaders, groups, officers, and members determine to reach new people and grow, with God's help nothing will stand in their way.

Principle # 2 *Disciple-making is most effective when focused on the oikos (natural networks) of existing Christians.*

In church after church, denomination after denomination across America, and around the world, God uses friends, relatives and associates as the primary means of reaching people. This has been the process, as we have seen, since the earliest days of the Christian church.

As we discussed in Chapter Two, webs of common kinship (the larger family), common friendship (friends, neighbors), and common associates (special interests, work relationships, recreation), are the means by which most people become Christians.

The fact that a great majority of people come to Christ and the local church through webs of relationships has important implications for your church. An effective disciple-making plan is one that builds on this solid foundation and allows God's love and salvation to flow naturally and intentionally over these bridges.

Here are eight important reasons why identifying and using natural networks of relationships should be the foundation for the outreach strategy of every church:

1. It is the natural way churches grow;
2. It is the most cost effective way to reach new people;
3. It is the most fruitful way to win new people;
4. It provides a constantly enlarging source of new contacts;
5. It brings the greatest satisfaction to participating members;
6. It results in the most effective assimilation of new members;
7. It tends to win entire families;
8. It uses existing relationships.

Principle # 3   *Disciple-making is most effective when based on, and permeated with, love and caring.*

"This is my commandment, that you love one another, as I have loved you. Greater love has no man than this, that a man lay down his life for his friends."[2]

I remember being part of a ten-month consultation project in the Middle East. I lived alone on the bottom floor of a five-story apartment building. It was a cold and wet January. After enjoying a nice dinner at a corner restaurant, I

walked home through a light snowfall, and retired for the
night.

About 3:00 a.m. I woke to a slight twinge in my stomach
. . . it was trying to tell me something. Laying in that small,
hard bed I had an uneasy feeling that it concerned the potato
salad which I had eaten for dinner. By 4:00 a.m. my stomach
was no longer hinting at a potential problem. It was coming
right out and announcing: "Friend, we have a problem!" By
5:00 a.m. there was no doubt that I was the full-fledged
recipient of a fine case of food poisoning. I kept telling
myself, "It's okay. Think about something else. It will go
away," all the while secretly hoping against hope. But, as
seasoned foreign travelers know, food poisoning has a habit
of not going away without a fight. I spent the remainder of
the early morning plodding a path between the bed and the
bathroom. By daybreak I could barely move. Sometime after
noon, with much effort, I dressed and walked down the snow-
covered street to a public telephone, called the office and
told them my situation. I said I would not be in; in fact the
way I felt, I was lucky to be alive!

The acute sense of isolation I felt as I stumbled back to
my apartment is still vivid in my mind. There I was, half a
world away from my home and family, in a strange city where
I could not even speak the language. I was cold, wet,
miserable, and felt that if I died no one would ever know, or
care. I trudged slowly back to the apartment, stumbled
through the entryway outside my room, and collapsed back
in bed.

Some hours later I was awakened by the loud electric
doorbell. Bzzzzz . . . Bzzzzz. I walked slowly to the door. On the
other side of the twenty-foot indoor entryway which led
outside the building, I saw two of our American team
members with whom I worked, standing in the snow waving
to me. They had come in response to my earlier call. In my
bathrobe I walked over and opened the door to a blast of
cold air and snow. My friends had cooked up a thermos of
vegetable soup, walked the two miles from their apartment to

mine on that cold, snowy night to deliver their spirit of concern and a thermos of soup. It was one of the most touching moments of my life. Their caring and concern for me seemed unrepayable. I couldn't express what it meant. I wasn't alone. Someone cared. I was loved. What a world of difference it made!

Caring for people is a key distinctive and quality of effective disciple-making . . . a genuine expression of God's unconditional love. "For God loved the people of the world so much that He gave His only Son so that everyone who believes in Him should not be lost, but should have eternal life."[3] God's love for His children is beyond question: "You must let the children come to me; you must never stop them. The kingdom of heaven belongs to children like these."[4] Effective disciple-making calls for each Christian who is a recipient of Christ's great love to become a channel through which that love can flow to those whom Christ wants to give life eternal.

CARING—Allowing God's love to flow through you to people, especially those in your network of relationships.

God has seen fit to communicate His love to non-Christians through His representatives. "The person who loves God loves his brother also."[5] Christians are commissioned to represent Christ; and Christ's greatest quality is that of love.[6]

The translation of Christ's "love" into tangible, specific action is the process of "caring." Caring is spending time with a person. Caring is building a stronger and closer relationship. Caring is helping in a time of need, doing things for someone else that you would do for yourself. "We know that we have crossed the frontier from death to life because we love our brother . . . My children, let us love not merely in theory or in words—let us love in sincerity and in practice."[7] Caring is loving. And we are called to love and care for one another.

"But I have called you friends; for all things that I have heard of my Father I have made known to you. You have not chosen me, but I have chosen you, that you shall go and bring forth much fruit, and that your fruit should remain . . . These things have I commanded that you love one another."[8]

Principle # 4   *Disciple-making is most effective when each Christian has a part in responding to the Great Commission.*

Anyone can do it! Any church member who can identify an unchurched friend, relative, neighbor, or associate can be a disciple-maker. As we have seen, the average church member has between seven and nine friends and relatives outside of Christ and the Church.[9] Newer Christians and members of newer churches average twelve. Older Christians and members of older churches can list an average of four unchurched friends/relatives. If a church of 200 members had an average of six unchurched friends/relatives per member, the prospect list of potential disciples would be 1,200! Even if there were an overlap of 200 people, the church would still have identified 1,000 people, by name, who would be some of the most receptive people anywhere in that community. Since the members with those relationships are usually the best "bridge" to their web, making disciples becomes the concern of *each* member as they communicate God's love to these particular people.

This wide-spread lay participation in disciple-making not only contributes to enlarged church outreach, but also results in considerable side benefits. One such benefit is in the Christian maturity among participating church members and throughout the corporate spiritual life of the Body. Individual Christians actively involved in the Great Commission discover a sense of purpose and meaning to their Christian life. Perhaps for the first time they feel they are

making a significant contribution to the cause of Christ.
Being part of such a cause immeasurably improves the self-
image of a person and gives an important sense of spiritual
self-worth. Productively participating in making disciples
certainly responds to that spiritual need.

How does spiritual maturity and growth occur in a
Christian's life? What actually contributes to a growing,
developing, maturing Christian? Is it daily prayer, regular
Bible study, frequent participation in Sunday School and
worship? Certainly these are all important. Yet often we
assume that spiritual growth occurs only in the context of
such activities. Actually, it doesn't. In fact, when personal
growth-oriented concerns make up the entire experience of
the Christian life and the church's programming, the result is
to actually stunt the individual's spiritual growth and
development. Why? Because participation in the very thing
Christ desired most of His disciples—to make the Good
News known—is completely ignored. "Christ-likeness" can
hardly be an achievable goal if there is no participation in the
basic reason for Christ's mission.

It may be something like searching for happiness. People
seldom find it by looking for it. They find happiness as a
result of involving themselves in a task that is fulfilling and
satisfying. Happiness is the *result*. Spiritual maturity is much
the same. The secret may not be in the search, but in the
result; the result of commitment to a greater task of "bringing
forth much fruit"—of making disciples.

Christ said it best: "Unless a grain of wheat falls into the
ground and dies, it remains alone; but if it dies, it bears much
fruit. He who loves his life in this world shall lose it; but he
who hates his life in this world shall keep it for eternal life."[10]
Participating in the process of disciple-making may be as
worthy for its role in the maturity of the Christian as it is in
reaching the non-Christian. A Christian remains spiritually
immature if he/she is not actively involved in the greatest task
the Master called us to do.

Being part of productive disciple-making is great spiritual

therapy! It can spark the most weary of Christians and churches with a new flame of enthusiasm and excitement as they see new people—their friends and relatives—come into the joyful experience of the Christian life. Effective disciple-making is a stimuli for unfathomable renewal in personal growth and corporate church morale.

Below is a graph of a typical church, prior to their involvement in reaching their "oikos."

It shows (A) the total membership of the church, (B) the number of members involved in one or more church activities, (C) the number of those members involved in activities of service to existing Christians and existing church structures, and (D) the number of involved members participating in outreach toward non-Christians. You may want to develop a graph like this in your own church.

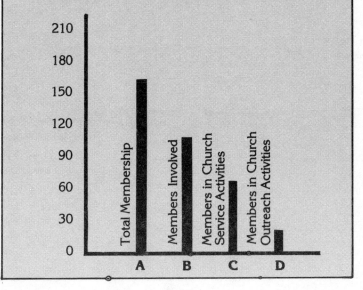

Two and a half years after this church raised the priority for making disciples, the same chart looked like this:

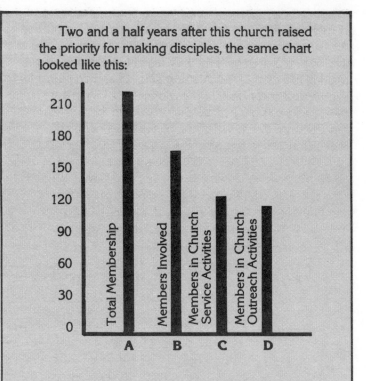

* Some members were involved in both church "service" activities and church "outreach" activities (identifying and reaching those in their web).

Notice that in addition to the growth in total membership of thirty-seven percent (160 to 220), there was a sixty percent increase in total involvement (100 to 160), and a major increase of members involved in outreach activities (15 to 110) who had become involved in making disciples through the church. In the next two or three years this church will see substantial new growth as members' relatives and friends come to Christ, who, in turn, begin to reach out to their webs.

Principle # 5   *Disciple-making is most effective when it is a "team effort."*

I remember as a boy venturing down a narrow, four-foot wide dirt tunnel which gradually descended deeper and deeper into the ground. A friend and I thought it would be an exciting adventure to find out where it led. I led the way. On hands and knees we made our way down the incline. About ten feet from the tunnel entrance we began a slight turn to the left, and soon the comforting light of day was lost. We groped along against the darkened walls down farther and farther. I felt more and more isolated and alone. What if the tunnel collapsed? We would be stranded. No one knew where we were—they would never find us. I can vividly remember the hollow, empty sense of being alone. We both decided the "adventure" was not worth the anxiety or potential consequences—and we backed out!

I remember a similar feeling of isolation, apprehension, and separation when I was part of a witnessing/calling program. A friend and I were given a list of names and addresses, and sent out to call. I led the way. But as we left the security of the church and other members, I felt like I was crawling down a deep, dark hole. We were removed from the comfortable security of the Body and its members, and sent to call on people I had never seen . . . I didn't know . . . and who might be very hostile. If things went according to plan, we would present our memorized steps and ask the person for a decision. If the people were not receptive, it was probably the last time they would hear from us. And if they were not home, we would leave a door-hanger and depart. Regardless of the outcome, the responsibility resting on our lone shoulders weighed heavily. I wondered how could I, in a ten-minute call, represent all that Christ and my church meant to me? All the needs Christ could meet in a person's life? The joy of communion, fellowship, and growth with God's people? How could we communicate such things with total strangers . . . strangers who may not even be asking the questions we were going to answer? I felt like my tunnel was

about to collapse. I was isolated, even from my own church. I
wanted to back out!

There must be a better way!

God hasn't planned for us to be isolated. He has given us
a community of brothers and sisters. A community whose
whole is greater than the sum of its parts.

Why is a "team effort" more productive for disciple-
making than any one individual's effort?

One reason is because each member has been given
different gifts to "build up the Body."[11] The concept of
spiritual gifts is as old as the New Testament. Peter notes that
each Christian has been given a gift.[12] Paul says, "Now
concerning spiritual gifts, brethren, I do not want you to be
uninformed."[13] Numerous other passages throughout the
Bible directly or indirectly refer to the fact that Christians are
given gifts to use in the service of Christ's Body.

While a detailed study of spiritual gifts will bring many
new insights into the Christian life, the important insight for
disciple-making is that the variety of gifts God has given his
church should play a central part in communicating the
Gospel. While no one person has all gifts, each Christian has
at least one gift to be used in the Body. Effective disciple-
making, therefore, means using your own gift, and then
supplementing yours with other gifts in a team effort to build
the Body. All gifts can be used, and should be used, to help
the church grow.

Consider how the gifts of others in your church can be
used to complement your own.

A second reason why a team effort will be more effective
in disciple-making is that the more and varied the contacts a
non-Christian has with the Body, the more completely that
person will see Christ.

One reason that traditional one-to-one evangelism may
sometimes be unfruitful is that the non-Christian looks at a
"Christian" and says, "Well, if that's what a Christian is, I
certainly don't want to be like that." Perhaps that one
Christian person is the only picture the non-Christian has

ever had of the enormously varied changes and spiritual fruit Christ produces in the lives of Christians.

Unfortunately, for many church members, when it comes to exemplifying Christ in their lives, well . . . they come through as being only too human. "Dull of hearing" and "children unskilled in the word of righteousness"[14] is the way the Bible puts it. While a Christian is a new creature, in the sense that Christ is the new center of his being, he still carries many imperfections. Often the imperfections in the Christian's life are the part which a non-Christian sees, and on that basis rejects the invitation to the Christian life. Therefore, in our desire to portray the love of Christ, the greater number of experiences a non-Christian has with the variety of members which make up the Body of Christ, the more likely he/she is to see through the human short-comings of specific Christians and see the wholeness that Jesus Christ brings to His people.

A third reason why a "team effort" is more productive in disciple-making within one's *oikos,* is that on a practical level, these non-Christians *have to* make new Christian friends in the church or they won't stay! Research indicates that in most cases, the new decisions who soon "drop out" of active church involvement never made new friends in that church. Evangelism which does not include this important "friendship factor" will result in much loss of labor.[15] Disciple-making is most effective when it is a team effort.

Principle # 6 *Disciple-making is most effective when it is church-centered.*

The more distant evangelism is from the local church, the less "fruit" that remains; the closer evangelism is to the local church, the more "fruit" that remains. An effective strategy for disciple-making revolves around the local church. It is energized through the local church. The results accrue to the local church. The process of disciple-making has the church at the center of the evangelistic focus, and builds on the vast resources available through the Body.

Often, if evangelism is ineffective in actually making new disciples, the problem can be traced to the method of presentation. Non-Christians need an opportunity to accurately perceive and understand God's love and grace . . . as seen through the larger Body of Christ. Effective disciple-making should regularly introduce unchurched friends and relatives to the great variety of ways God works in people. The insightful children's poem "The Blind Men and the Elephant" is an excellent analogy of the need to help non-Christians experience the totality of Christ's love through his Body.

The Blind Men and the Elephant
By John Godfrey Saxe

There were six men of Hindustan,
To learning much inclined,
Who went to see the elephant
Though all of them were blind,
That each by observation
Might satisfy his mind.

The first approached the elephant
And happening to fall
Against his broad and sturdy side,
At once began to bawl,
"God bless me, but the elephant
Is very like a wall."

The second, feeling of the tusk,
Cried, "Ho! What have we here?
So very round and smooth and sharp,
To me 'tis mighty clear,
This wonder of an elephant
Is very like a spear."

The third approached the animal
And happening to take
The squirming trunk within his hands,
Thus boldly up did spake,
"I see," quoth he,
"The elephant is very like a snake."

The fourth reached out an eager hand
And felt about the knee,
"What most this wonderous beast is like,
Is mighty plain," spoke he,
" 'Tis clear enough the elephant
Is very like a tree."

The fifth who chanced to touch the ear,
Said, "Even the blindest man
Could tell what this resembles most,
Deny the fact who can,
This elephant, I say to you,
Is very like a fan."

The sixth no sooner had begun,
About the beast to grope,
Then seizing on the swinging tail
That fell within his scope,
"I see," quoth he,
"The elephant is very like a rope."

And so these men of Hindustan
Disputed loud and long,
Each in his own opinion,
Exceeding stiff and strong,
Though each was partly in the right,
They all were in the wrong.[16]

What does it mean . . . "church-centered disciple-making?"

While the church's unique role in *The Master's Plan* is examined in detail in Chapters 6 and 7, the following functions of the church are central to effective disciple-making:

- The church initiates disciple-making through an intentional strategy;
- The church trains its members in effective disciple-making;
- The church coordinates the resources of the Body for effective disciple-making;
- The church creates programs and ministries for effective disciple-making;
- The church structures accountability into disciple-making;
- The church incorporates new disciples into the Body.

Principle # 7   *Disciple-making is most effective when unique needs and individual differences are recognized and celebrated.*

"I have, in short, been all things to all sorts of men, that by every possible means I might win some to God. I do this all for the sake of the Gospel."[17]

A significant barrier which often stops many people from becoming Christians is one we actually create ourselves. It grows out of the assumption that all people come to Christ in the same way . . . that they all have the same needs and the same problems, and that our simple memorized steps to eliciting a Christian decision will respond to their need.

The fact is that people come to Christ in many different ways, for many different reasons. And for Christ to be considered as a viable alternative in anyone's life, the Gospel must be presented in ways that speak to those unique needs.

Effective disciple-making recognizes the unique

Why Do People Join the Church?

Different people join the church for different reasons. In an exploratory study, Edward A. Rauff, Director of the Research and Information Center for the Lutheran Council in the U.S.A., asked 180 people to respond to the question, "Why did you join the church?"[18] (Some interviewees indicated more than one reason for their decision.) Their answers fell into the following categories:

Family Relationships and Responsibilities.   The dominant reason thirty respondents gave for establishing a relationship with a church was to keep the family together and to strengthen family life. The pull of a family member made them look toward the church.

The Influence of Christian People.   Twenty-two said that they saw a difference in the quality of life of a friend, relative, neighbor, or co-worker, and then connected that difference in some way to the person's religious conviction or church membership.

A Church Visit, Program, Special Event, Sacred Act.   Nineteen recalled that when they visited a church for special occasions or were brought into some church programs, they felt called to a deeper awareness, reflection, or self-examination.

A Search for Community.   A friendly atmosphere made eighteen feel at home when they visited a church. It bespoke a relationship that was warmer and deeper than they had experienced in non-church groups. This warm welcome made a return easier.

Personal Crisis.   Seventeen felt they had lost control of their lives. Various events prompted a reordering of priorities and values and a reaching out to the church for help in meeting needs not previously experienced.

The End of Rebellion.   Fifteen said their decision

to join a church was made in response to a need to
take up a role that had been laid aside, a need to "go
home," and return to former values and principles.
The Influence of Pastors. For twelve interviewees,
the clergy were crucial in drawing them into a
congregational relationship. The one-on-one
interactions with clergy were milestones in the
spiritual journeys that ended in church affiliation.
God's Intervention. Twelve described their
turning toward the church as so sudden and
unexpected and so difficult to explain that it was "out
of the blue," an act of God. God's *kairos* was also
seen as a time of fulfillment, after earlier starts toward
some church relationship.
The Journey Toward Truth. Eleven of the
respondents pursued a personal and determined
journey toward truth, often in the face of resistance.
Square one, in some journeys, was a college course
in intellectual history or the chance reading of some
Christian author, or intense discussion with some
Christian apologist.
A Feeling of Emptiness. Eleven people who were
interviewed noted a "feeling of emptiness" although
they had "everything." An aching, long-festering
sense of hurt or sudden discovery of great loneliness
nudged them along their way toward the church.
The Response to Evangelism. Ten felt they had
been reached through the formal efforts of a
congregation that initiated an evangelism thrust
within the community. They cited the gentle, yet
persistent concern of Christians for their present
church affiliation.
The Reaction to Guilt and Fear. Ten of those
interviewed gave rather intense testimony that joining
the church freed them from a feeling of guilt and
insecurity and gave them an assurance of salvation.

differences of the friends and relatives in each member's web
(oikos). Consequently, the way God's love is communicated
is based on an understanding of these individual differences.
The following questions help clarify some of the differences
among non-Christians in a person's *oikos* which have an
effect on how God's love is communicated:

- What is the level and depth of my relationship with this
  person?
- What other Christians/church members does he/she
  know well?
- What are his/her understandings of Christianity? What
  are his/her misunderstandings?
- How receptive is the person to becoming a Christian?
- Would this person feel comfortable in our church
  (regarding such factors as age, marital status, race,
  ethnicity, socio-economic status, common interest?)
- Are his/her needs in areas our church can meet?

An understanding of the unique qualities and needs of
each member implies a unique approach in the disciple-
making process, an approach which will vary from one
person to another. While specific steps for reaching
individual web members will be discussed in detail later, an
important insight into effective disciple-making is that several
memorized lines will not suit every person in every situation.
A study of the Gospel reveals that Christ Himself was a
powerful demonstration of meeting people where they were;
addressing the unique needs of each person and presenting
the Gospel in a relevant and meaningful way. Compared to a
total stranger, church members involved in reaching their
web are better able to understand the individuality of each
person, the needs he/she may have, and the appropriate
ways to introduce the need-meeting alternative of Jesus
Christ and His Church.

Principle # 8   *Disciple-making is most effective when
Biblical insights and church growth research are integrated.*

Christ's parable of the talents provides one of many insights into His desire to see the church grow. In this parable the master was pleased with the servant who was given five talents and doubled his investment to ten. The master was equally pleased with the servant who doubled his two talents to four. To these two servants his reward was generous: "Well done, thou good and faithful servant." But to the servant who had been given one talent and had buried it until the master returned, the rebuke was strong: "Throw this useless servant into the darkness outside, where he can weep and wail over his stupidity."[19] The master expected and desired his servants to multiply the treasure he had left with them!

"Church Growth" is an emerging field of study that is searching for and finding answers to the questions of how a local church can effectively multiply its "talents" to result in new Christians and responsible church members. The principles of church growth are bringing renewed hope to churches concerned with reaching greater possibilities of ministry, outreach, and growth. Church growth principles are being successfully applied in churches across the country. Churches participating in *The Master's Plan for Making Disciples* are using a process built on solid biblical and theological concepts, as well as the insights of years of church growth research.

Church growth principles can help make disciple-making more effective in many ways. Did you know, for example, that church growth research has found that people in your web will vary, over time, as to their "receptivity" to the Gospel? Did you know it is possible to tell when they are most receptive to becoming new disciples? Or, did you know that the way a church member views the "process" of verbally sharing the Gospel has an important effect on whether the non-Christian responds? Did you know that the events in the first few months of a new Christian's life often determine whether that person will continue as an active member, or will lose interest and drop out?

There are many important new insights into how people

come to Christ and the church which creatively and consistently support the examples of Jesus and the early Christians, and provide us with a practical *process* to see the Great Commission come alive in our congregation and community. (Readers interested in pursuing the insights and understandings of church growth will find the most complete listings of growth resources available through The Institute for American Church Growth.[20])

Principle # 9 *Disciple-making is most effective as a natural and continuing process.*

Continuous disciple-making requires prudent stewardship of church members' time and energy. It requires an evangelistic process that renews rather than exhausts laity. It requires a process that is a natural part of life, rather than a contrived event. This sounds like a tall order for pastors and evangelism faithfuls who may have struggled for years to enlist "volunteers" in calling programs or evangelism training events.

When does disciple-making become a natural part of the Christian life?

1. When it builds on natural human relationships. A recent national survey asked the question: "What do you enjoy doing most in your spare time?" The answer, from seventy four percent of the people surveyed, was "spending time with family and friends."[21]

God made people to enjoy other people. He made the family and the relationships that result. In every human culture on earth the family (or extended family) is the basic organizational structure.[22] God uses this natural human network of family and friends to most effectively spread the Good News. *The Master's Plan for Making Disciples* builds on this foundation.

2. When it builds on the need to love and be loved. People, both Christians and non-Christians, need caring and love. *The Master's Plan for Making Disciples* responds to this need in the lives of both church members and the people in

their web of influence. In the disciple-making process,
Christians learn how to strengthen relationships with non-
Christians and communicate God's caring through their own
caring. "You should love your neighbor as yourself."[23] The
commission of Christ is to share His love and to make
disciples.

   **3. When it becomes part of the entire church
organizational structure.** Effective, continuous disciple-
making does not translate into a program to be adopted,
organized, and carried out by a few select members of an
evangelism committee or calling team. It becomes a *process*
which becomes a natural part of each organization in the
church Body. The women's circle, the Sunday School
classes, the choir, the home Bible studies are all able to
become involved in the disciple-making process. Ideally, if a
church member is involved in any church activity, he/
she will be confronted with and encouraged in the
opportunity to make disciples in that particular context.

   4. When it is self-perpetuating. Effective disciple-making
can't help but be self-perpetuating. Indeed, not only does it
continue, but the process naturally enlarges. It happens when
one person (in a member's web) comes to Christ and the
Body, and then that new member has his/her own web of
relationships of friends and relatives outside of Christ. As the
new Christian identifies those people and begins making
disciples, the growth and outreach process through the
church enlarges again and again.

   The Master's Plan for Making Disciples is a *process* of
church-centered evangelism that has significant implications
for you . . . and for each active member of your
congregation. You will discover that *The Master's Plan* holds
fresh insights and exciting new concepts for making
disciples.

   The Master's Plan is an important new way of looking at
disciple-making in and through the local church. It is a
strategy for making disciples that goes beyond a special
evangelism committee or trained calling team. It has the

potential for positively affecting every group and organization in the church. It is a process which builds on new research in church growth previously unavailable to designers of evangelism strategies. It is a process that builds on the natural "webs" of relationships which exist in every church. It is a process that can be a joyful experience for each participating member. And it is a process that promises significant new effectiveness in making disciples for you and your church.

Footnotes

1. Win Arn, "People Are Asking," CHURCH GROWTH: AMERICA, March/April 1979, p. 11.
2. John 15:12,13
3. John 3:16
4. Matthew 19:14
5. I John 4:21
6. See I John 4:16
7. I John 3:14-18
8. John 15:14-17
9. Charles Arn, Donald McGavran, Win Arn, *Growth: A New Vision for the Sunday School* (Pasadena: Church Growth Press, 1980), p. 81.
10. John 12:24,25
11. Ephesians 4:16
12. I Peter 4:10
13. I Corinthians 12:1
14. Hebrews 5:11-13
15. W. Charles Arn, "The Friendship Factor," CHURCH GROWTH: AMERICA, May/June 1981, p. 13.
16. Hazel Felleman, Editor, *Best Loved Poems of the American People* (Garden City Publishing Co., 1936), pp. 521-22.
17. 1 Corinthians 9:22-23
18. These interviews are published in *Why People Join the Church* (The Pilgrim Press, 132 W. 31st St., New York, N.Y. 10001) by Edward A. Rauff.
19. Matthew 25:30
20. Institute for American Church Growth (709 E. Colorado Blvd., Suite #150, Pasadena, CA 91101)
21. According to Syndicated News Report KFWB, Los Angeles, June 4, 1981.
22. Peter Hammond, *Cultural & Social Anthropology: Selected Readings* (New York, MacMillan, 1964), pp. 145-146.
23. Galatians 5:14

Seven Steps for Making Disciples

Pastor Austin and Chuck had just finished a lunch together. As they returned to the church and were walking back to the church office, Pastor Austin asked, "Chuck, are you witnessing to anyone at the present time?"

Chuck was not proud of his answer. "No, not really."

There was a pause in the conversation as the two entered the Pastor's study and sat down. "Is that because the people you relate to—your neighbors, your relatives, friends, people you work with—are already believers?"

"Oh, no," answered Chuck. "I don't think any of the people I work with are believers. Neither are my neighbors. And relatives, well, I'd say maybe half are Christians."

"And with how many of these unreached people do you have a fairly close relationship?" asked Pastor Austin.

"Well, I guess I'm on a first name basis or better with about nine or ten."

"So how are they responding to your witness?" asked the Pastor.

At first Chuck thought he had heard wrong. "Responding? Didn't you hear what I said, I'm not witnessing to anyone."

Pastor Austin's words were disturbing: "Oh, but you are. Even if it's not intentional."

"You mean . . . the way I act? The things I say? The things

"But you are witnessing to them, Chuck, even if it's not intentional."

I do? That's all part of my witness?"
Pastor Austin nodded.

●◄●◄●◄●◄●◄

Every day each of us comes in contact with unreached persons with whom we have on-going, established relationships. These persons are called our "extended family."

Extended Families

If you are a father or mother, you no doubt feel an important sense of responsibility for your family. God has given you oversight for their physical health, safety, personal growth, spiritual development.

But did you realize God has given you an Extended Family for whom you also have a responsibility? They are members of your *oikos*—your close friends, your relatives, and associates—who do not know Jesus Christ. The people in your Extended Family are those non-Christians with whom you have a unique relationship. In many cases you may be the only "bridge" God has to them.

EXTENDED FAMILY: A church member's close friends, relatives, and associates who are not presently in Christ and the Church.

To develop your vocabulary in *The Master's Plan*, it is helpful to understand the difference between two terms: *"Oikos"* and "Extended Family."

Your *oikos* is composed of the people in your circle of influence—both Christians and non-Christians.

Your Extended Family, on the other hand, are the persons in your *oikos* who are not presently in Christ and the Church.

▶◀▶◀▶◀▶◀▶

Chuck Bradley considered his own Extended Family; those people he knew who were not presently Christians.

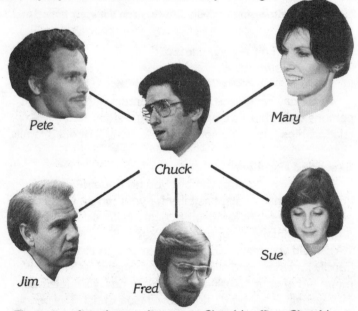

There was Jim, the art director at Chuck's office; Chuck's younger sister, Mary, who is getting a divorce; Pete, Chuck's next door neighbor; Fred, a friend at the gym where Chuck

works out twice a week; and Chuck's cousin, Sue, who lives a few miles away. Chuck saw each of these people frequently and enjoyed a mutually respected relationship with them. Yet none were Christians.

◆◀◆◀◆◀◆◀◆◀

So, how do you begin such a significant adventure as seeing those in your Extended Family come to Christ and the Church? Here are six important steps:

1. Identify Your Extended Family.

Analyze the regular contacts you have with people in your day-to-day life. Consider the people in each of the following groups: common kinship, common friendship, and common associates.

Those people who are related biologically or through marriage constitute the *common kinship* area of your Extended Family. One person's immediate family may be composed of a spouse and children. For another, it may include parents, brothers, or sisters. Other family members, such as cousins, aunts, uncles, in-laws, nieces, nephews, and grandparents may be part of an Extended Family.

Close friends are also part of your Extended Family. Through *common friendship,* you can identify people whom you regard as confidants; those you trust; those with whom you share plans and experiences, joys and sorrows. These are friends with whom you regularly communicate in person or by phone. Neighbors whom you know on a first-name basis are part of your Extended Family. Those you invite over for a backyard barbecue or social event, those you look forward to being with, are all part of the *common friendship* segment of your Extended Family.

The *common associates* area of your Extended Family may include people at work (or school) with whom you rub shoulders daily. Perhaps you enjoy coffee or eating lunch together. You share family news, talk over current events, and discuss matters of mutual interest pertaining to your work. Also in the *common associates* part of your Extended Family may be people with whom you do civic work or are involved in special clubs or projects. Perhaps you solicit funds together, or work on a committee, or share a mutual concern for your city and its quality of life.

Identifying and listing those six, eight, or ten people who comprise your Extended Family is an important first step in seeing them come to Christ and the Church.

2. Develop a Personal Profile of Each Extended Family Member.

Franklin D. Roosevelt made it a point to become a personal friend to every dignitary he met. Before the foreign leader came to visit, the President would study the person's hobbies, special interests, and areas of personal concern. When the diplomat and the President met, they first talked on an official, political level. But then the conversation often changed. The President would praise the diplomat for any special achievements he had made, direct the discussion to the diplomat's own hobbies or interests, and listen attentively as the person spoke. Through expressions of genuine interest, Roosevelt built friendships that endured a lifetime.

Knowing a person on a level beyond biographical details of age, marital status and occupation is part of effective disciple-making. The more we can understand the interests, concerns, and needs of our Extended Family members, the deeper and more substantial our relationship with them will be.

What do you know about the members of your Extended Family? What is each one's personal background? What do they do in their spare time? What are their attitudes toward various subjects? How is their family life and what concerns do they have in that area? Are they happy in their job? What important events are they experiencing in their life?

What do you know about the spiritual dimension of lives of the members in your Extended Family? What is their previous religious experience? What knowledge do they have about the Bible? What do they understand (or misunderstand) about the Christian life? What attitudes do they display concerning "Christian things"? Are they open or antagonistic to discussing spiritual matters? Do they have any Christian friends?

Also, note why you think the person is not a believer. Has he/she heard the Gospel; been invited to accept Christ; perceived no need for a relationship with Christ; chosen another religious lifestyle?

You may not know the answer to all these questions. If not, this is an important place to begin the disciple-making process—simply getting to know the person in a more meaningful way.

3. Focus Your Efforts.

As you review the list of names in your Extended Family, you may want to identify several people with whom you have a natural, warm relationship. They are people with whom you get along well. You enjoy doing things together and have a variety of common interests. They may be people who would enjoy being with your friends from church. These people should be ones you feel to be potentially receptive to the Gospel and who could easily find a home in your congregation.

The number of people you can focus on may differ according to the amount of time you give to consciously sharing God's love. A busy executive, for example, may have time to work effectively with only one or two people at a time, whereas a retired person could easily focus on six or more non-Christians in their Extended Family.

Chuck Bradley identified three members of his extended family to focus on—Pete, his next door neighbor, Mary, his sister, and Fred, his friend from the gym.

Pete is married but has no children. His wife is six months pregnant. Pete's favorite recreational pastime is fishing. He repeatedly invites Chuck, but so far Chuck has never gone

His neighbor, Pete, had often invited Chuck to go fishing, but so far Chuck had never gone.

with him. Pete's church background is "zero."

Mary, Chuck's sister, is getting a divorce after seven years of marriage. They have no children, and she is twenty-eight years old. Mary, at one time, was active in church, but after her marriage to a non-Christian, she became inactive. Mary is currently unemployed and has a high school education. She worked a few years prior to her marriage, but has acquired no real marketable skill.

As for Fred, Chuck sees him regularly down at the gym where they both work out twice a week. They enjoy sharing information about their respective families, jobs, and the weather, but never see each other outside of the gym.

4. Develop a Disciple-Making Plan

Scripture's admonition to plan carefully is particularly applicable to making disciples: "Any enterprise is built by wise planning, becomes strong through common sense, and profits wonderfully by keeping abreast of the facts."[1]

Introducing non-Christian friends and relatives to Christ, and directing their attention to the opportunity of new life, demands our best efforts. Yet often we tend to run ahead in our evangelistic methods without first considering insights that might increase our effectiveness.

Our disciple-making plans need to begin with meeting people at their point of need. Paul said, "I have become all things to all people, in order that I might win some."[2] Effective plans for communicating the Gospel need to recognize the unique ways hearers perceive and personally relate the Good News to their lives and needs.

Christ's approach to introducing the Kingdom to people was highly individualistic. It was often based on events with which the listener could readily identify. He met people on their own ground. He respected them as individuals with unique interests and needs. He asked the woman at the well for a drink of water. He told stories about sowing and harvesting to people who understood such things.

Because the disciple-making plan which you develop for your Extended Family members is so important, the next chapter (Five) will be entirely devoted to practical suggestions in developing an effective plan for each person non-Christian in your *oikos*.

5. Work the Disciple-Making Plan.

As you begin to implement the steps of your disciple-making plan (Step 4), be sensitive and aware of the events in your Extended Family member's life. There could be a right time and a wrong time, a right way and a wrong way to communicate Christ's love.

Here are some suggestions for developing skills in effective communication with Extended Family members:

A. *Attentive Listening.* A prominent theologian once said, "The first duty of love is to listen."[3] Almost everyone is born with the capacity to hear. However, the ability to listen must be deliberately learned and cultivated through practice.

Becoming skilled in attentive listening is a valuable skill for every lay person concerned with effective disciple-making.

Chuck had been trying to really listen to his friend Fred's ideas and opinions. Chuck found listening to be hard work since he enjoyed talking, even to the point of monopolizing many conversations. But as he and Fred worked out in the gym, Chuck was beginning to listen. The result was a deepening of their friendship as Fred began sharing more of himself with Chuck.

What is "attentive listening"? It is concentrating on what the other person is saying rather than letting our mind race ahead to what should be said next. Attentive listening is putting ourselves in the other person's shoes. It's seeing things from their perspective rather than our own. Attentive listening is empathetic, comprehending, and non-judgmental.

Another element of attentive listening is your body language—eye contact, an encouraging nod, an understanding smile. A study in communication effectiveness showed that words alone carry only about seven percent of the communication message. The tone of delivery contributes thirty-three percent. Yet the non-verbal aspects—the body language—comprise fifty-five percent of the communication process.[4]

Attentive listening has no "hidden agenda." Listening is not geared toward turning the conversation to spiritual matters at the first opportunity. Rather, attentive listening seeks to understand the non-Christian friend's dreams and ambitions; to discover his needs and his problems; and to develop a level of understanding that builds a mutual respect and personal empathy.

B. Relating to Needs. God's love is the greatest need-meeting resource on earth. Be alert to the unique areas of need in your Extended Family members.

A close and meaningful relationship includes mutual sharing of experiences . . . happiness, sadness, success, failure, irritation, disappointment. It is around the personal experiences of life that the importance of faith and fellowship in the church often become apparent. Points of need in your own life, or the lives of your Extended Family members, provide a natural point for demonstrating your Christian faith, relating your experiences to theirs, and discussing the solution Christ has provided you. "I will mention the loving kindness of the Lord, and the praises of the Lord, according to all that the Lord has bestowed on us. . . ."[5]

Following their workout, Chuck and Fred were talking in the gym dressing room. The conversation turned toward their families and Fred began to talk about his daughter. "Tina's mixed up with kids that Joan and I think are headed for trouble and she just won't listen to us. Frankly, we don't know what to do, or where to turn."

"That can be pretty tough," said Chuck sympathetically. "Peer pressure can really be powerful. We had similar problems with Karen."

"What did you do about it?" asked Fred.

"Well, we've tried to let Karen know that we love her, and that God loves her." Chuck continued, "I also think that becoming more involved in the youth group at our church has been a big help."

Chuck went on to briefly describe the family counselling program available through his church.

The next day Fred checked out the church's counselling program and soon he, his wife, and their daughter were involved. All because Chuck had been able to honestly identify with Fred at his point of need.

C. Identifying Receptive Periods. God's love and caring is especially appropriate during significant changes in lifestyle (such as marriage, birth of a child, new job, retirement, etc.), or incidents of stress in our Extended Family members' lives (death of a spouse, divorce, family crisis, injury, etc.). These times are called "periods of transition." A period of transition is a span of time in which a person's or family's normal, everyday behavior patterns are disrupted by some event that puts them into an unfamiliar situation. The more recent the "transition-producing event" in the person's life, the more receptive he or she will be to a new lifestyle which includes Christ and the church.[6]

Consequently, it is important to stay in close touch with your Extended Family members and respond immediately in a time of transition. Being aware of these periods of transition in our non-Christian friends, and responding by showing them the caring love of Christ and the Church, can be an important step in seeing them become new Christian disciples.

Receptivity-rating Scale

The scale on page 91 indicates different events, in approximate order of their importance, which have an effect in producing periods of personal/family "transition."[7] The numbers on the left indicate the importance of the event relative to other transition-producing events. Various events may compound on each other when an individual experiences more than one incident over a relatively short period of time. The higher the number, the more receptive the person to the Gospel. For example, someone who was just married and is also having trouble with their boss will be more receptive than if either event had occurred separately. Also, the larger the number or accumulation of numbers, the longer the period of transition will last and the more intense it will be.

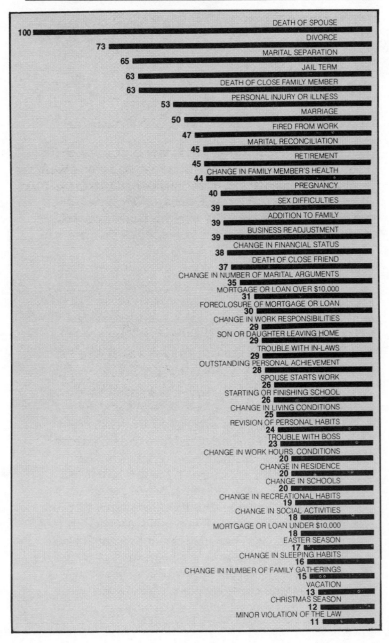

DEATH OF SPOUSE
100

DIVORCE
73

MARITAL SEPARATION
65

JAIL TERM
63

DEATH OF CLOSE FAMILY MEMBER
63

PERSONAL INJURY OR ILLNESS
53

MARRIAGE
50

FIRED FROM WORK
47

MARITAL RECONCILIATION
45

RETIREMENT
45

CHANGE IN FAMILY MEMBER'S HEALTH
44

PREGNANCY
40

SEX DIFFICULTIES
39

ADDITION TO FAMILY
39

BUSINESS READJUSTMENT
39

CHANGE IN FINANCIAL STATUS
38

DEATH OF CLOSE FRIEND
37

CHANGE IN NUMBER OF MARITAL ARGUMENTS
35

MORTGAGE OR LOAN OVER $10,000
31

FORECLOSURE OF MORTGAGE OR LOAN
30

CHANGE IN WORK RESPONSIBILITIES
29

SON OR DAUGHTER LEAVING HOME
29

TROUBLE WITH IN-LAWS
29

OUTSTANDING PERSONAL ACHIEVEMENT
28

SPOUSE STARTS WORK
26

STARTING OR FINISHING SCHOOL
26

CHANGE IN LIVING CONDITIONS
25

REVISION OF PERSONAL HABITS
24

TROUBLE WITH BOSS
23

CHANGE IN WORK HOURS, CONDITIONS
20

CHANGE IN RESIDENCE
20

CHANGE IN SCHOOLS
20

CHANGE IN RECREATIONAL HABITS
19

CHANGE IN SOCIAL ACTIVITIES
18

MORTGAGE OR LOAN UNDER $10,000
18

EASTER SEASON
17

CHANGE IN SLEEPING HABITS
16

CHANGE IN NUMBER OF FAMILY GATHERINGS
15

VACATION
13

CHRISTMAS SEASON
12

MINOR VIOLATION OF THE LAW
11

The antithesis of this receptivity principle is also a factor in your disciple-making activities. That is, Extended Family members in a personally stable situation, with few complications or unusual interruptions in their life, are generally not as open to becoming disciples. Often the only way to reach an Extended Family member not presently open to the Christian faith is to be alert to a "period of transition" when their receptivity will increase, then respond in love by sharing Christ's love.

D. Appropriate Timing. A fourth important point in effectively responding to your Extended Family member is that of timing. *When* you communicate God's love and the Christian experience can be as important as *what* you communicate. The most effective witness is at the appropriate moment. For example, when Fred explained his difficulty with their daughter to Chuck in the gym, it was an appropriate moment for Chuck to relate how his faith guided him in similar circumstances. The timing was ideal for Chuck to communicate the church's support and suggest a Christian alternative to Fred for an important question he was facing.

E. Understandable Language. Sharing the realities and benefits of Christ in everyday language, in the context of our everyday experience, gives a credibility and relevance to the Christian faith that is uniquely important to an Extended Family member. As you mention your faith, and the difference in your life because of it, speak in words and phrases the person will understand. Sharing your own experience helps your non-Christian friend sense that your relationship with Christ has an important influence on your attitudes and actions in everyday circumstances. Paul told the Christians at Colossae: "Make the most of your chances to tell others the Good News. Be wise in all your contacts with them. Let your conversations be gracious as well as sensible, for then you will have the right answer for everyone."[8]

Each of the areas mentioned above will help you understand and respond more effectively to the unique concerns of your Extended Family member.

6. Pray Regularly and Specifically for Each Extended Family Member.

"The earnest prayer of a righteous man has great power and wonderful results."[9]

Prayer must be at the very heart of the disciple-making process. The importance of regular prayer for specific members of your Extended Family cannot be overemphasized. It is a crucial part in the process of making disciples. If this vital step is overlooked, the chances of ever seeing your Extended Family member come to Christ and the church are slim.

After you have identified each person in your Extended Family by name, as part of your daily prayer life, pray for each of them specifically and for their needs. Ask God for the opportunity to let His love for them be experienced through you.

Do you remember the definition of "caring"? "Allowing God's love to flow through you to people, especially those in your network of relationships."

Through prayer, we express our specific concerns for each person in our Extended Family. We should pray according to their unique needs, attitudes, and situations. It may well be that the person in our Extended Family has never before been held up to God in prayer. What a thrill to be the first one to have that privilege! And it is impossible to talk daily with the Lord about a person and not become genuinely concerned about them and aware of caring/ sharing opportunities you have with them.

One of the most important activities of a church organizationally committed to helping members disciple their Extended Family is regular prayer offered by Christians for each other's Extended Family members. Rev. Wayne McDill, a pastor in Portland, Oregon, has correctly observed that

"greater strength can be brought to bear in your prayers as
you involve others in praying for your friend."[10] Jesus
provided a promise at this very point: "If two of you agree on
earth about anything that you may ask, it shall be done for
you by My Father who is in heaven."[11]

Each lay person involved in making disciples should pray
not only for the non-Christians in his/her own web, but for
specific people in other members' Extended Families.
Sharing prayer concerns, asking God for a sense of
awareness to opportunities that arise, and thanking Him for
answered prayer are important parts of each person's role in
making disciples.

7. Accept Your Accountability to Others and to God.

A final major step in the disciple-making process is to
meet regularly with other Christians similarly involved in the
process. As you discuss goals and individual experiences in
regular meetings, you will find an important sense of support,
fellowship, and accountability.

No member's caring relationships with Extended Family
members will be quite identical. Thus, sharing individual
successes and failures can provide rich learning experiences
for every church member involved. One person's insights
sharpen another's understanding. And the probability of each
member continuing as an active disciple-maker is vastly
increased when he/she is part of such a regular group.

In these meetings, members share their prayer concerns
for each person in their Extended Family. These concerns
become the subject of intercessory prayer for the entire
group. Likewise, experiences of answered prayer are shared
with the group and expressed in praise and thanks to the
Lord.

Praying for fellow church members is an encouraging
and enabling aspect of these times together. Thanking God
for the opportunity to demonstrate His love and Word
through a caring witness helps members keep their disciple-
making ministry at the forefront of their Christian lives. As

Christians ask God for guidance, wisdom, insight, and sensitivity, they build a confidence and self-worth in being ambassadors of God's love. These times of prayer together are a mutual expression of dependence, anticipation, and assurance of God's ability to direct His people.

Church members may want to become prayer partners with one another. Each agrees to pray for his/her partner and the people in his/her Extended Family. The disciple-making process is strengthened immeasurably as each Extended Family member is daily held up by others before the Lord in prayer.

Your Opportunity . . .

A denominational leader has observed, "If you and I are to enjoy our disciple-making opportunities, we need to take our witness out from behind the walls of our church building and into our neighborhood. . . . Life's greatest satisfactions are found as we witness to what Christ is doing in our lives while we engage in the normal activities of the day."[12]

Is it possible to see the lives of friends, relatives, and associates really change as they encounter the miraculous love of Christ? Can you, as an "ordinary layman," have a meaningful and purposeful role in reaching these people with Christ's love? The answer is a resounding, affirmative "YES." You can do it! In fact, you are probably *the best* person able to show these Extended Family members the burden-lifting power of Jesus Christ.

Footnotes

1. Proverbs 24:3,4
2. I Corinthians 9:22
3. Paul Tillich in *The Friendship Factor* (Augsburg Publishing House: Minneapolis, 1979), p. 109.
4. Albert Mehrabian, "Communicating Without Words," in PSYCHOLOGY TODAY, September 1978, p. 53.
5. Isaiah 63:7

6. W. Charles Arn, "How to Find Receptive People," *The Pastor's Church Growth Handbook* (Pasadena: Church Growth Press, 1979), p. 143.
7. Adapted from Holmes-Rahe Stress Test, University of Washington Medical School.
8. Colossians 4:5,6
9. James 5:16
10. Wayne McDill, *Making Friends for Christ* (Nashville: Broadman, 1979), p. 96.
11. Matthew 18:19
12. Roland E. Griswold, *By Hook and Crook* (Charlotte: Advent Christian General Conference of America, 1981), p. 97.

How to Reach Your "Extended Family"

It was late afternoon and Diane Bradley had invited her friend Judy for a quick cup of coffee. This had become a regular ritual since Judy returned to work. Judy was recently divorced and is the mother of three small children. She's working again, not because she wants to, but because she has to.

"Diane it's so frustrating to work as a clerk-typist in the same office I once managed."

"Judy, that must be hard," replied Diane sympathetically.

"And all because I took ten years out to start a family." Judy brought her cup to the kitchen sink. "Well, enough of this crying on your shoulder. I've got to get home and relieve the sitter. Thanks for the coffee."

"You're welcome, Judy. Maybe next week we could get together for lunch."

"I'd like that."

After Judy had gone, Diane breathed a silent prayer for her divorced friend. She asked particularly for wisdom in knowing the best ways to show Judy that God loved her.

You will remember, in the steps to disciple-making we discussed in the previous chapter, that Step Four was to "Develop a Disciple-Making Plan" for the members of your Extended Family.

"Diane, it's so frustrating to work as a clerk typist in the same office I once managed," said Judy.

One of the most important steps in reaching friends and relatives in your Extended Family will be developing an appropriate and effective strategy for introducing those people to Christ and His Body. Here are some key insights that will help you develop an effective plan to communicate God's love to each person in your Extended Family.

1. Caring.   Your most important role, as a witness to the people in your Extended Family, is personifying Christ's love. Christ's love is communicated through your caring.

Here is a major principle in effective disciple-making: *"God's love is best seen and experienced by others through our love."*

Consider the burden-lifting implications of this concept! The traditional requirements of a "good" witness (verbal fluency . . . extrovertive personality . . . tenacity . . .) become less important in an effective witness than simply being an open channel through which God's love can be expressed

and experienced by those in your Extended Family. Think of
it . . . you become the channel for God's love! Exciting? Yes!
Possible? Absolutely!

God's great love for these potential disciples, and His
desire to express that love, is seen throughout Scripture. As
He first loved us, we express our love for Him through loving
others . . .

"For I was hungry and you fed me; I was thirsty and you
gave me water; I was a stranger and you invited me into your
home; naked and you clothed me; sick and in prison, and
you visited me. Then these righteous ones will reply, 'Sir,
when did we ever see you hungry and feed you? Or thirsty
and give you anything to drink? Or a stranger, and help you?
Or naked, and clothe you? When did we ever see you sick or
in prison, and visit you?' And I, the King, will tell them, 'When
you did it to these my brothers, you were doing it to me.' "[1]

Scripture graphically illustrates what love for Christ
entails. It is a basic, down-to-earth involvement with people in
need. The response is to be personal . . . the response is to
be caring. The people in your Extended Family may not
require clothing, food, or water. But they do have real needs.
Responding to the void of loneliness, frustration, or despair
demands a personal investment of genuine caring.

David Augsburger, in his book *Caring Enough to
Confront,* observes that caring people ". . . dare to be present
with people . . . and to stand with people where they are
hurting."[2] "Caring people look for the opportunity of
affirming, of encouraging, of helping release others to
become all they can be in Christ."[3] Caring for the members
of your Extended Family is an ongoing process. Does one
meal satisfy a hungry person for life? Does one visit to a
lonely person cause their loneliness to disappear? Caring
requires an investment of time and patience. Paul Cedar
notes "You simply cannot love another only on your
schedule. You must be willing to be available when the other
person needs you. Availability is an essential ingredient of
authentic love."[4]

One writer has suggested a helpful way of understanding Christ's perfect love, by substituting the name "Jesus" for the word "love" in Paul's great chapter 13 of I Corinthians. "Jesus was patient, kind, never jealous, boastful or arrogant. He did not act unbecomingly, did not first seek His own interests, was not touchy; did not keep account of wrongs suffered nor gloat over the hardships of others. His greatest joy was seeing truth come to life. He accepted all that people said or did to Him, trusted all who approached Him, believed the best for all who despaired. He set no limits for what He could endure. His concern, respect, and compassion could outlast anything."[5] Christ is a model for our caring relationships with Extended Family members. The caring aspect of making disciples reflects God's very nature: "God is love."[6]

Diane Bradley and Judy Miller were sitting in the kitchen of the Bradley home one afternoon having another cup of coffee . . .

"Without your help and friendship, Diane, I don't think I could have survived these last three months. When Tom walked out on me I was devastated," said Judy.

"Isn't that what friends are for . . . to help each other?"

"I guess . . ." Judy replied. "But no one's ever been this kind to me before—not even my own family." After a pause she continued, "Diane, do you really like me . . . as a person?"

"You know I do," Diane replied.

"Yes . . . but I also know that you've got some kind of religious faith . . . even though you've never talked much about it. You go to church on Sundays. You've got Bibles and religious books lying around. Diane, I've got to know. Are you being nice to me because you're trying to convert me?"

Diane was somewhat taken back by the question.

"Judy, my friendship is not some kind of bait to get you to join my church, or become a Christian. But my faith does have something to do with my caring for you."

"I knew it," said Judy, "you have got an angle."

"Does that mean you'll still be my friend, even if I don't want your religion?"

"Please, Judy, hear me out," said Diane earnestly. "My faith isn't just in a religion, it's in a person—Jesus Christ. And He has radically changed my life. There was a time when I could never love someone without, as you call it, an 'angle.' But because of Jesus Christ in my life, I'm beginning to."

"Does that mean you'll still be my friend even if I don't want your religion?"

"Judy, of course I will."

◄►◄►◄►◄►◄

Diane was exemplifying an important insight: our caring and friendship with others must be *unconditional*. It is not the bait of a religious trap. Nor is it the scheming means to an ultimate end. Unconditional caring is a reflection of God's unswerving and unrelenting love. If a friend were to say, "I don't want anything to do with your religion," should your caring be any less than before? Do you think God's love is any less for those who reject Him? If anything, God's concern is even greater. How many people have once rejected His love and then later, perhaps in a time of need, responded and are now active reproducing Christians? Caring must be genuine and unconditional, and not depend on how the person responds to spiritual overtures.

"Unfortunately," observes Paul Little in his book *How to Give Away Your Faith,* "many non-Christians today are suspicious of all Christians because of a previous contact with a 'friendly' religious person who had ulterior motives. Some non-Christians refuse to listen to a single word about our Lord until they're sure we'll be their friends, even if they reject Jesus Christ. We must love each person for himself."[7] Christ wants His lost children found. We should not take it upon ourselves to close the door on the relationship that God has (through us) with these Extended Family members. Caring must be genuine, long-term, and unconditional.

2. Strengthening Relationships.   Your disciple-making effectiveness is enhanced where strong relationships exist with members of your Extended Family. The Apostle John writes, "Dear friends, let us practice loving each other, for love comes from God and those who are loving and kind show that they are the children of God."[8]

What person does not enjoy the companionship of a loving, caring friend! A strong and growing relationship between you and your Extended Family member contributes immeasurably to allowing the Holy Spirit to speak to that person.

In *The Friendship Factor,* McGinnis says, "It is no accident so many important encounters occurred between Jesus and His friends when they were at the table. There is something almost sacramental about breaking bread with one another."[9] Invite your friend to attend a special event that you both will enjoy. Drop by his/her home with something from your garden, workshop, or flowerbed. Perhaps you could make it a point to have lunch once a week with the person in your Extended Family, or seek him/her out for a coffee break conversation. Do you know of any special needs your friend

Strong relationships come with shared experiences.

has mentioned which could be a point of relationship building, such as helping lay a brick walk, hanging drapes, or painting the house? Strong friendships come with shared experiences. "Working shoulder to shoulder strengthens a relationship even when few words are spoken."[10]

As your relationship grows, expect your Extended Family member to also respond to your needs and reciprocate caring initiatives. Friendship is not a one-way affair. The close relationship will be as meaningful to you as to your Extended Family member. The joy and fulfillment which comes from being with friends and giving of yourself is one of the emotional highlights of life. Enjoy it!

Scripture speaks repeatedly of joy as an integral part of a relationship, both with the Lord and with one another. "If we are living in the light of God's presence, just as Christ does, then we have wonderful fellowship and joy with each other."[11] As you look at your Extended Family members through God's eyes—made in His image to be part of His family— take pleasure in loving those people and directing their attention toward God's love. Wayne McDill points out that "as an expression of our love for them, we endeavor to communicate the vast resources available through Christ and His Church, and what God can do to make life a meaningful and rewarding experience".[12] This selfless concern results in a unique sense of inner joy and fulfillment. Each of us has the privilege of being an ambassador of Jesus Christ and His love.[13]

Here is an important distinctive that should be pointed out. The idea of "friendship evangelism" is not new in evangelism circles. A number of programs have been built on an approach that encourages Christians to "make friends to win souls." It would be a mistake to interpret the emphasis of friendship and caring found throughout *The Master's Plan* to be one of manipulation or scheming to get a decision. There is a significant difference between the *reason* for a relationship (to get a "convert"), and the result of a caring relationship (often a new "disciple"). Build your friendship with sincerity and unconditional caring.

A helpful research study[14] shows the importance of friendship in the process of becoming a new disciple. The study, reported in CHURCH GROWTH: AMERICA Magazine, identified two hundred forty (240) new Christians presently active and involved in their churches. In addition, a second group of 240 people were identified who could be classified as "drop-outs" (they had made a recent decision but had since lapsed into inactivity). A third group of 240 people were identified who had been presented with the Gospel message, but had chosen not to make a positive decision. In individual interviews with these 720 people, each was asked to classify the person who had presented the Gospel into one of three categories: "Friend," "Salesman," "Teacher." The results provided some startling conclusions: The people who saw the church member as a "friend" were almost all now Christians and active in their churches (94%). On the other hand, those people who saw the church member who presented the Gospel as a "salesman" often made an initial

As you spend time with your Extended Family member, your sense of values and purpose in life naturally surfaces.

decision, but soon dropped out in large numbers (71% later dropped out). Finally, those who saw the church member as a "teacher" generally tended to not respond at all (84% said "no thanks"). The implications are clear. The non-Christian person who perceives your relationship as one of a "friend" is far more likely to eventually respond to Christ's love than the person who sees you either as a "teacher"—instructing on doctrine, sin, and morality; or as a "salesman"—manipulating them toward an eventual decision.

Your greatest resource in developing a meaningful and caring friendship is in simply being yourself—natural and unmasked. The phrase "I'm not perfect, just forgiven" reflects a healthy attitude in recognizing the shortcomings each person has. The unique benefit of the Christian life is in the strength and support from a source greater than ourselves. When your Extended Family member understands this simple truth, it may change his/her entire attitude toward faith and life in Christ.

She and Judy were home when Diane's sister called with the news that their parents had been in an automobile accident, and their mother had been killed.

As you spend time with your Extended Family members, your sense of values and purpose in life naturally surfaces. In his book *Power in Praise,* Carothers observes that if we grumble and complain as bitterly as our non-Christian friends over the many little upsetting incidents of the day, others conclude that our faith does no more than occupy an hour of our time Sunday morning.[15] How do you react to delays or difficulties on the job; to emergencies; to everyday encounters? Do you respond in a way that causes non-Christian friends and relatives to see a difference which suggests the quality of your life in Christ?

Diane Bradley discovered the insight of simply being yourself following a stressful event in her own life: an event which her friend Judy Miller happened to witness. She and Judy were at the Bradley home when Diane's sister called with the news that their parents had been in an automobile accident, and their mother had been killed.

Judy watched as Diane sat down and started to cry. After a moment she asked, "Doesn't it help . . . I mean, your faith?"

"Sure it does," answered Diane. "I know I'll see Mom again. I have that hope. But, Judy, being a Christian doesn't take away the pain."

Somehow Judy had assumed that Christians never experienced pain or grief. Sharing that time of sorrow with Diane was a turning point in Judy's life. Realizing that Christians are not isolated from reality was a big step forward in Judy's decision to become a disciple.

3. Using Other Members of the Body. A third important consideration in your plan to successfully communicate God's love to your Extended Family members, is to use the unique resource of your church. In effective disciple-making the local church is a central part of the process. In fact, disciple-making simply cannot be effective outside the context of the local church. One obvious reason is that the goal is to make *disciples;* and a disciple is one who is actively involved and incorporated into the life of a local church—namely yours.

One important resource for disciple-making found in your church is other church members, particularly your close friends. Encouraging and building personal relationships between your Extended Family members and other Christian friends in your church is a highly effective way of introducing your non-Christian friends to the variety of ways Christ works in the lives of people. No person, other than Jesus, has ever been a perfect example of the Christian life. If you are the only Christian your Extended Family member knows, then his/her perception of the incarnation of Christ in a person's life is limited to what that person sees in you.

What a unique new perspective to sharing God's love . . . introducing Christ to your Extended Family member through the people in your church. And how much more accurate an introduction than one simple explanation of who and what Christ is, from one single source.

This "cross-pollinization" between your Extended Family members and various Christians in your church adds a dynamic dimension to the disciple-making process. On one hand, it provides you, as a disciple-maker, with support from other members. In turn, you become part of other church members' disciple-making activities as you build relationships with their Extended Family members. The process adds to the effectiveness of disciple-making, to the common concern of church members for other non-Christians, and to the accountability of church members concerning the people in their Extended Family. The process of communicating God's love through the lives of other Christians takes a significant burden of responsibility off the back of just one person. Christians can look to the Body and its members for support in making disciples.

How do you help such relationships flourish between your Extended Family members and others in the congregation? Informal social gatherings at your home, or group outings to special events can include both Christian and non-Christian friends. The church may want to sponsor a series of special events or workshops of interest to non-Christians. The purpose of the events would be to provide an opportunity for building relationships between Extended Family members and other church members. Christians introduced to other members' friends should make it a point to be as friendly and caring as they would hope other church members would be to their own unreached friends. An "Extended Family consciousness" should begin to develop which encourages church members to build warm and potentially on-going relationships with non-Christian persons met through other church members.

You may want to use present church programs, classes, and activities to introduce your Extended Family to others in the church. A special Sunday School elective class might be of interest to your friend, or perhaps a worship service where a particular message would be relevant. Church-sponsored social events are excellent opportunities to bring a non-

Christian friend and introduce him/her to friends in the
church. Another approach could be to enlist your Extended
Family members in an on-going group, perhaps a home
Bible study or a weekly lunch meeting, with some friends
from church.

*Chuck's neighbor Pete loved fishing. To strengthen their
relationship, Chuck accepted Pete's invitation to go fishing.
And the second time they went out, Chuck arranged for
Andrew, a church member who loved fishing, to go as well.*

*As for Fred, his friend at the gym, Chuck arranged some
bowling dates with Fred and two men from the church to
make up a foursome.*

*Chuck encouraged his sister Mary to attend a church-
sponsored seminar on "Coping with Divorce." Since Mary is
in need of a job, Chuck introduced Mary to two young career
women from the church who are now helping Mary study for
her real estate license. In addition to the employment
prospects, the three women are becoming good friends.*

*Through these various contacts with the ministries and
people from his church, three members of Chuck's Extended
Family are learning more about Christ's love and how He is
exemplified in the lives of others.*

From the church perspective, providing opportunities for
members to build relationships with the Extended Family
members of others is a major step in effective disciple-
making. Activities sponsored by the church for building such
relationships may not directly present the Gospel message,
but they meet important needs and establish meaningful
contacts which communicate the love of Christ to potential
disciples. (Chapter Six is devoted entirely to the church's
important role in disciple-making.)

4. Enhancing Your Witness. As you think and plan
how to communicate God's love to your Extended Family,
the question naturally arises, "But what do I say?" To find the

answer to that question, let's turn to the Bible.

In searching Scripture to answer the question, "What do I say," one is impressed that there is no one simple formula that was used. Every situation was different. Indeed, the Bible presents a wide variety of illustrations as to how people came to faith. Noted scholar P.T. Forsyth has observed of the New Testament model, "there was no universal theological formula. There was not an orthodoxy, but certainly there was a common apostolic gospel, or kerygma."[16]

Jesus, in teaching His disciples to be fishers of men, used many different models. From Nicodemus, the religious ruler who was told he needed to be "born again,"[17] to the woman of Samaria who was offered water of eternal life,[18] to the thief on the cross who asked only to be remembered when Christ came into His kingdom.[19] Each situation presents different needs, portrays different relationships, uses different words, brings a different response. Each situation was unique.

However, while there was not one formula, there were common denominators of the Gospel presentations which appeared again and again in biblical models. What are they?

The assumption—man's sinful nature. The teachings of Jesus, the Apostles, the early church all assume the common sinfulness of mankind. Because of man's sinful nature, the Gospel embodies a call to repentance and faith. Scripture abounds with the recognition of the sinfulness of mankind: "All of us like sheep have gone astray. Each of us has turned to his own way, but the Lord has caused the iniquity of us all to fall on Him."[20] "Indeed, there is not a righteous man on earth who continually does good and who never sins."[21] "All have sinned and come short of the glory of God."[22] ". . . His laws serve only to make us see we are sinners."[23] "If we say we have no sin, we are only fooling ourselves and refusing to accept the truth."[24]

The focal point—Jesus Christ. People in the New Testament did not respond to a series of theological propositions. They responded to a person—Jesus Christ. "Come and see . . . we have found the Messiah," said

Andrew.[25] "Come, see a man . . . is not this the Christ?" asked
the woman at the well.[26] "We have met the man spoken of in
the law," Philip told Nathaniel.[27]

The target for witness—responsive people. Jesus told His
followers: "As you enter his house, give it your blessing . . .
but if no one will welcome you, or even listen to what you
have to say, leave that house or town, and once outside it,
shake the dust of that place from your feet . . ."[28] Jesus was
instructing His disciples to identify receptive people and
communicate the Good News to them.

Throughout the New Testament we are instructed to
focus on people who are willing to listen and respond:
"He that has ears to hear, let him hear."[29] "Turn your eyes
unto the fields that are already white unto harvest."[30] "The
seed sown on good soil is the man who hears and understands . . ."[31]

In the book *Growth: A New Vision for the Sunday School,*
the authors note: "Paul's strategy for growth was to find and
win responsive people . . . people whom God had prepared."[32]
Sharing the Good News with responsive people whom God
had prepared is a common denominator of New Testament
strategy.

The starting place—the person's need. The message was
relevant because it spoke to the person's need. Jesus'
ministry of healing focused on people's needs . . . then their
healing . . . then their following of Christ. "They that are whole
need not a physician, but they that are sick."[33] The Christian
commitment one sees in Scripture is not based on a series
of theological propositions to believe in, but on a faith that
makes people whole. "Then He said to her, 'My daughter,
your faith has made you whole.' "[34]

The instrument of God—people. God uses people, in
most cases, to bring other people to Himself. Conversions do
not take place in a vacuum. Philip was there to interpret the
Scripture for the Ethiopian. Peter was there to help Cornelius.
Paul was there to help Lydia. When people in the New
Testament came to faith, they came through the

influence and help of others.

The proclamation—The "kerygma." There were important essentials that comprised the first Good News proclaimed by the early church. The *kerygma* (a Greek noun meaning 'proclamation' or 'preached message') was the earliest Gospel Christ's apostles took out to their world.[35] Archibald Hunter reviews the essentials of this *kerygma:* "The prophesies are fulfilled . . . the Messiah has come. He is Jesus of Nazareth, the servant of the Lord . . . who was crucified according to God's purpose, was raised from the dead on the third day, is now exalted to God's right hand, and will come in glory for judgment. Therefore, repent, believe this Good News, and be baptized for the forgiveness of your sins and the gift of the Holy Spirit."[36]

This message was preached by all the apostles. At Pentecost, Peter preached, "Therefore let all the house of Israel know for certain that God has made Him both Lord and Christ."[37] Paul proclaimed that through Christ, "God was manifest in the flesh, justified in the Spirit, seen of angels, preached unto the Gentiles, believed on in the world, received up into glory."[38] In I Corinthians Paul outlines a summary of the *kerygma,* and then comments, "Whether, then, it is I or they (Peter, James, John, and the rest), this is what we all proclaim."[39] The basic elements of the *kerygma*— the message—were proclaimed with the goal of persuading the hearers to repentance, faith, and baptism.

The movitation—love. Christ's entire life and ministry was a personification of God's unconditional love. The apostles and early church continued to emphasize this all-encompassing love. The rapid spread of the Gospel must have been in large part due to their desire to see others share in such extraordinary love.

The method—dialogue and interaction. The Ethiopian posed questions to Philip about the Scripture passages he was reading.[40] Paul asked Jesus for a confirmation of His identity.[41] The Philippian jailer asked, "What must I do to be saved?"[42] Cornelius asked the angel for an explanation of his

vision, and asked Peter for an explanation.[43] The woman at
the well asked Christ of His identity.[44] Nicodemus,[45]
Zacchaeus[46] . . . all interacted and had the opportunity to
question, discuss, and consider the claims of Christ.

The goal—repentance/conversion. John the Baptist
called for repentance.[47] Jesus' teaching and preaching
demanded repentance.[48] Peter's instructions required
repentance.[49] Paul's message required repentance.[50]
Repentance is an important step, from the biblical viewpoint,
in the conversion process. Repentance involved a change of
mind and heart; a turning "from." The other side of
repentance is conversion. It is a person's turning of
allegiance to God in obedience and faith. In the turning and
new lordship in life, God regenerates and gives eternal life.[51]
'Re-birth,' 'new life in Christ,' 'obedience to the faith,' 'hearing
the Word of the Gospel,' 'hearing the Word,' 'believed,'
'believed and were baptized . . . the Scripture uses many
terms to describe a person who has moved from death to
life, from doubt to faith, from sin to salvation.

The result—baptism and identification with the church.
In the New Testament the rite of incorporation into the Body
was baptism. Baptism was a crucial part of becoming a
Christian. "In fact," observes Smalley in *Conversion in the
New Testament,* "the New Testament knows nothing of
coming into the Body by faith only. It was by faith and
baptism. Baptism was the accompanying act of obedience
and confession, and without baptism, a believer did not enter
the early community of faith."[52]

Sharing Your Faith: Six Suggestions. Here are some
specific suggestions to help you in verbally sharing your faith
with others, especially those in your Extended Family. They
are built on the biblical examples and models of the verbal
part of being a witness.

1. *Be sensitive to the spiritual needs and receptivity of
those in your Extended Family.* Skills of listening, of empathy,
of identification, of relating the Gospel and the church to

WHAT IS THE GOSPEL?

To five basic questions, the Gospel message gives penetrating answers . . .

Who am I? Every person, at some point in his/her life, has asked, "Who am I? What is my identity?" God has anticipated this question and at the very outset of the Bible, in its earliest pages, he addresses it. Indeed, when we open the Bible, we are face to face with the great truth of creation. "And God created man in His own image." Here is His answer: we have been made in the image and likeness of God Himself! We can find our identity in this reality . . . that I have been created for a relationship with God.

How can I be made fit for God's presence? Being made acceptable to Him has to do with what Jesus Christ did when He took my guilt and shame and made it His own. He received on Himself the judgment I deserved. The Bible calls this the redemptive, atoning work of Christ and it leads to "justification by faith." By this we mean God accepts me "in His Son," cleansed by the blood of His sacrifice and clothed with the righteousness of Christ. I am thereby declared righteous and am fit for God's presence and fellowship. All this is God's response to man's quest for acceptance.

Can my life be changed? The Gospel also touches on another basic question, "Is there any possibility of my character being transformed? Must I always be pushed around by habits I can't control?" The Good News of the Gospel is that, through what the Scriptures call "sanctification," through the in-working of God's Holy Spirit, I can put off my old self. I can put on the new. I do not need to remain the person I once was. Jesus Christ liberates. Jesus Christ sets men free. I can be conformed to the image of Jesus Christ. That, indeed, is good news!

To whom do I belong? The Good News says, "You belong to a community, the community of God's people, the Body of Christ." If you have received Jesus Christ and experienced the new birth, then you have the privilege—indeed, the obligation—of relating yourself to all those who have similarly reached out for Jesus Christ. You belong to them and they belong to you. Together we share a common life. Prior to coming to Christ, we are alone, as solitary individuals. But after we come to Christ, we find we are members of a family, the family of God. And as we participate in the life of a local congregation, we become enriched and strengthened in our Christian life.

Is there hope for the world? Shall the world always know poverty, war, oppression, and injustice? Christians are to be the salt of the earth. They are to stand against the rottenness of the times. They are to be Christ's presence in the midst of people. They are to work for social justice and for the improvement of the human condition. But more, Christians are to look for the second coming of Jesus Christ. This is the great hope of the church. There is coming a day unlike all other days. And before that day ends, the nations shall know the presence of the Lord and the knowledge of the glory of the Lord "as the waters cover the sea." Then righteousness shall reign. Then sin shall be forever gone. Then all shall witness the new heaven and the new earth.

So, the Good News of the Gospel provides identity, acceptance, transformation of character by the Holy Spirit; it provides community, belonging and hope for the world! What Good News we have to bring! The Gospel is the one message which can satisfy the total yearning of human hearts, and meet the total needs of our world.

relevant needs will be of great value in knowing when and how to share the Good News. Asking questions will help you determine where your friends are in their spiritual journey.

2. *Be open to the Holy Spirit's direction.* In most cases the Holy Spirit uses people to bring other people to faith. Isn't it exciting that He has chosen you to be a witness of His eternal grace? Isn't it affirming that He believes in you enough to open doors where you can communicate the faith? Closing yourself off to His leadership is unproductive. Opening yourself by saying, "Here I am, Lord, send me" is the door that leads into enlarged ministry, usefulness, blessing and joy.

3. *Be able to verbalize the reasons for the hope that is within you.*[53] You should be able to testify clearly to your own faith. Describe the events that brought you to repentance, faith, and into the church. Be confident in expressing "why" and "how" Jesus is Lord in your life. Some people find help in writing out their testimony and memorizing it. Others rehearse it with a friend. Whatever means you use, be able to share your personal experience clearly, concisely, and in words understandable to a non-Christian.

4. *Know the "kerygma"—the Gospel of the Kingdom.* Be on solid speaking terms with the basics of your faith—man's sin; Christ's incarnation, death, and resurrection; repentance; faith; etc. The more appropriate Scriptures you know, the more comfortable you will feel. While proclaiming the Gospel is more than simply reciting Bible verses, having a grasp of Scriptures concerning His love and how one enters into the Kingdom of God is an important part of the process.

5. *Identify your own spiritual gifts, then supplement yours by using other gifts in the Body.* The apostle Paul understood this great truth when he said, "I planted, Apollos watered, but God causes the growth . . . Now, he who plants and he who waters are one, but each will receive his own reward according to his labor."[54] The Bible is clear that God gives gifts to His Church—to His people—and that their use is to build up the Body.[55] Each member of the Body is given different gifts. We do not all have the gift of evangelism—that

special ability to "share the Gospel with unbelievers in such a way that men and women become Jesus' disciples and responsible members of the Body of Christ."[56] If you have the gift of evangelism, by all means use it. But if you have the gift of hospitality, prayer, witness, teaching, pastor, wisdom, giving, mercy, helps, or something else, these also can be used for making disciples. In fact, all gifts are given, as Paul says, "to build the Body." Use not only your gifts, but those of the Body to support you in your witness.

6. *Realize that evangelism is not complete until the person is incorporated into the Body.* The end goal of effective evangelism is that the new Christian becomes a disciple and responsible member of the church. As you think of your Extended Family members, your disciple-making plan will include incorporation into the Body. Incorporation goes beyond just formal membership. Effective incorporation, as you will see later in this book, has a variety of dimensions; but the end result is that people are active parts of God's family, using their gifts joyously in His service.

5. Provide for a variety of exposures. As we just noted, each church member should be able to express comfortably the meaning of Christ in his/her own life to a non-Christian friend. A dialogue between two friends on the subject of the church and Christianity would include sharing one's personal experience on the subject. There is an important credibility in such sharing between two respected friends.

At the same time, as you plan ways to communicate God's love to the members of your Extended Family, realize that there are additional ways to communicate the message . . . perhaps more persuasively. The pastor, a special evangelistic film, a guest teacher or speaker, or a church member with the gift of evangelism may be able to present the Gospel in a more compelling way than you. Actually, most people who end up as active Christians and responsible church members have heard the Gospel more than once from more than one source, prior to making their decision for Christ. One particular research study found that those who were vital Christians and active church members had heard the Gospel presented an average of 5.8 different times before they made their Christian commitment.[57] This fairly high number of exposures to the Gospel among the group of active Christians was in sharp contrast to the number of times the Gospel was heard among people who made a decision but soon became inactive. On the average, church dropouts heard the Gospel only twice prior to their decision.

This leads to some important implications about communicating the Good News to your Extended Family members. People who eventually come to Christ and become active members of your church need to have enough exposures to the Gospel (and the *implications* of their life-changing decision) to feel they are making a reasonable decision—one they can live with in the months and years ahead.

To illustrate this important disciple-making principle, suppose you were thinking about purchasing a house. You probably wouldn't buy the house after only one or two brief presentations. You would study the market, have the house appraised, look at the neighborhood, schools, taxes. You would talk with other people, probably "sleep on it" for a while, look at alternatives, and finally, after you felt you understood the implications of your contemplated action, you would make the decision to purchase. So it is—or should be—with the life-changing decision confronting your non-Christian friend. Church growth research shows that the person who makes a Christian decision on the spur of the moment (perhaps at the conclusion of an emotional public meeting or a high-pressure "manipulative" presentation) is not likely to continue as an active disciple. There is much more hope for the person who has had a number of exposures to various elements of the Gospel, has seen Christianity demonstrated in the lives of others, and has considered the important implications of his/her decision.[58]

How do you provide for this important variety of Christian

and Gospel exposures for your Extended Family member?
Again, the unique and irreplaceable resources of the local
church come into play. . . .

As mentioned previously, bringing non-Christian friends
to church-sponsored events serves to both enlarge their own
view of Christ in people's lives, and to build friendships with
other Christians. But bringing your Extended Family member
to church-related events also allows the person to hear and
see other aspects of the Gospel. A "full blown" evangelistic
message and invitation is not required (or perhaps even
desired) at every church-sponsored event. A brief devotional
or prayer at the beginning or end of the event satisfactorily
serves the important function of providing the non-Christian
with a growing understanding and perspective of the Gospel.

This need for a variety of evangelistic exposures means a
church needs to provide adequate opportunities for
members to bring their non-Christian friends and relatives.
Worship services and Sunday School classes may be one
means in this process. But other events and material may
need to be designed to provide such support to the church
member. Films, printed material, special outings and social
events, home Bible studies, inquirer's classes, special interest
seminars can be used as ways to provide exposure to the
Good News. The key insight is not *what* the particular means
of communication is, but rather the *number* and *variety* of
exposures—how many times and from how many sources
has your Extended Family member been exposed to a
portion of the Good News through the church? The more
exposures he/she has, the better the chances of that person
understanding the love of Christ and becoming a responsible
church member. Look for ways to help bring this about.

6. Patience.   Exercising patience and consistency is
vitally important in the disciple-making process. Remember
that each person in your Extended Family is at a different
level of development. Not all fruit ripens at the same time.
Arthur Glasser, noted theologian in the field of church
growth, observes, "Human hearts are not all the same. Some

are very open; some are quite resistant because they are cluttered up with all sorts of things, so that they have no room for the Lord."[59]

As you are involved in the process of making disciples, it is important to let the Holy Spirit do the work, and not take it upon yourself to force a decision. Paul Little has rightly observed, "None of us can play God for another person. We can't determine the stage of the Holy Spirit's work in his/her life. It may take several years for him/her to come to the Savior and a long period of disinterest may precede his/her decision. For Christ's sake, we must love them nonetheless. It is the Holy Spirit, not we, who converts an individual."[60]

Trying to manipulate a non-Christian into a "decision," through a series of dramatic appeals or pre-conceived steps, results in a staggering number of "dropouts" in a short period of time. The nation-wide "I Found It" campaign by Campus Crusade, several years ago, resulted in many thousands of decisions following a presentation of the "Four Spiritual Laws." Research studies conducted a year later, however, indicated that only 3 out of every 100 decisions made could be found in a local church, and half of those in a new church came through transfer.[61]

The "new life" of the unfortunate people who are victims of a "quick sell" decision rarely becomes a reality. Such "instant evangelism," as Samuel Southard puts it, produces many "stillborn babies."[62]

Helping people understand the implications of God's unconditional love, in their own time frame and their own life situation, requires patience and consistency. It is a process that should not be hurried. View the act of expressing God's love to members of your Extended Family as a continuing part of your everyday life, a process in which you willingly enter into a long-term commitment of your time and energy for seeing your friend come to Christ and the church.

Keith Miller, looking at his own personal life in communicating God's love to non-Christians, comments, "As I began to read the New Testament accounts, I saw that

Christ almost never went out of His way to help anyone. He seems to have walked along and helped the people in His path. He was totally focused on doing God's will and going where God led Him. But He never failed to help the people He met along the way while going where God directed Him. This made for an amazing steadiness and spiritual economy in His direction and ministry. This one change in my perspective made witnessing not a program but a part of a way of life."[63]

Chuck Bradley and his neighbor Pete had been enjoying a growing friendship. Before Chuck identified Pete as a member of his Extended Family, the two had had only a casual "Hello, how are you?" acquaintance. Chuck knew that Pete's wife was expecting her first baby in a few months, and that Pete's favorite recreation was fishing. Beyond that, they had seldom talked about anything more than the weather.

But as a result of his commitment to making disciples, Chuck had made it a point to strengthen his friendship with Pete. He had gone fishing with him and had even helped Pete paint his house. Twice he had invited Pete to go on fishing trips with men from the church who shared Pete's fishing passion.

On the day he became a new father, Pete dashed over to tell the news to Chuck and Diane. Later, when the two were alone, Pete spoke confidentially: "You know, Chuck, after my son was born last night, I never felt happier. But it was the damnedest thing, I found myself bawling like a baby. Wasn't that stupid?"

"I don't think it was stupid at all, Pete," Chuck replied. "I remember I did the same thing when Karen was born."

"No kidding?" Pete asked.

"That's right."

"You know, being a father is kind of new to me," Pete said. "And I've been doing a lot of thinking. I really need to clean up my act. You know having a kid, that's a heavy responsibility."

"You know, being a father is kind of new to me," Pete said.

Actually, this turn of events caught Chuck without much to say. As he thought about it later, he sort of "blew it." Pete was receptive and would have listened had Chuck shared how his faith helped him as a father. But all Chuck said was, "Hey, Pete, our church has a really good class for new parents. It deals with a lot of things that are really helpful to new parents. You and Marlene might really get something out of it. Plus, you'd meet couples who are going through the same thing for the first time."

But Chuck's "missed opportunity" didn't prove to be all that serious, because Pete and his wife joined the class for new parents . . . which was their first contact with the church.

Later, Pete and his wife began attending other church related activities, including Sunday worship services. In time both of them made commitments to become disciples of Jesus Christ. As Chuck looked back, he saw that almost one year had elapsed from the time he first identified Pete as a member of his Extended Family and the date of Pete's Christian commitment.

The way in which Pete came to faith and subsequent incorporation into the church is an excellent example of The Master's Plan *in action. As the Apostle noted, before the harvest, there is planting and watering that must be done. And then, in the right season, "God gives the increase."*[64]

CLARIFYING YOUR CONVICTIONS

Inherent in the disciple-making activity is the assumption that both you and your church hold important basic convictions. Here are four questions each potential disciple-maker should consider, then answer. Clear, strong convictions will increase one's effectiveness in the process of making disciples:

1. *What do you really believe?* What are your basic convictions as a Christian? Can you express, in simple and plain English, what you believe about God? Christ's love? Sin? Salvation?

2. *Why did you become a Christian?* What was the reason you personally made your commitment to become a Christian? Is being a Christian something you would wish on your best friend or worst enemy?

3. *Why are you a member of your church?* Are there benefits from being active in your church? What are they? Is membership in your church something you regularly celebrate? Or do you feel it is usually a burden?

4. *Do you understand your commission?* Is the idea of a "Great Commission" (for you) something you really believe? Does it apply to you as much as to any other Christian, or is it basically an idea for ministers and missionaries?

If you are not satisfied with your answers, do something about it. If you feel comfortable with your conviction base, you are ready to put faith into practice.

Footnotes

1. Matthew 25:35-40
2. David Augsburger, *Caring Enough to Confront* (Scottdale: Herald Press, 1980), p. 127.
3. Ibid., p. 138.
4. Paul A. Cedar, *Seven Keys to Maximum Communication* (Wheaton: Tyndale House Publishers, 1980), p. 71.
5. David Augsburger, op. cit., p. 138-139.
6. I John 4:8
7. Paul E. Little, *How to Give Away Your Faith* (Downers Grove: InterVarsity Press, 1966), p. 52.
8. I John 4:7
9. Alan Loy McGinnis, *The Friendship Factor* (Minneapolis: Augsburg Publishing House, 1979), p. 54.
10. Ibid., p. 55.
11. I John 1:7
12. Wayne McDill, *Making Friends for Christ* (Nashville: Broadman Press, 1979), p. 53.
13. Paul E. Little, op. cit., p. 53.
14. Flavil R. Yeakley, Jr., "Research for the Growing Church," CHURCH GROWTH: AMERICA, January/February 1981, p. 10.
15. Merlin R. Carothers, *Power in Praise* (Plainfield: Logos International, 1972), p. 117.
16. P.T. Forsyth, *The Principle of Authority* (Independence: Independence Press, 1952), p. 127.
17. John 3:3
18. See John 4:14
19. See Luke 23:42
20. Isaiah 53:6
21. Ecclesiastes 7:20
22. Romans 3:23
23. Romans 3:20
24. I John 1:8
25. John 1:41
26. John 4:29
27. John 1:45
28. Matthew 10:12-14
29. Matthew 13:9
30. John 4:35
31. Matthew 13:23
32. Charles Arn, Donald McGavran, Win Arn, *Growth: A New Vision for the Sunday School* (Pasadena: Church Growth Press, 1980), p. 72.
33. Matthew 9:12
34. Mark 5:34
35. See C.H. Dodd, *The Apostolic Preaching and Its Developments,* Hodder and Stoughton, 1936, for a comprehensive analysis of this subject.
36. Archibald Hunter, *Introducing the New Testament,* 3rd Edition (Philadelphia: Westminster Press, 1972), pp. 23-24.

37. See Acts 2:36-38,41
38. I Timothy 3:16
39. I Corinthians 15:11
40. See Acts 8:27-29
41. See Acts 9:1-9
42. See Acts 16:25-35
43. See Acts 10
44. See John 4:5-30
45. See John 3:1-21
46. See Luke 19:2-10
47. See Matthew 3:2
48. See Mark 1:15 and Luke 13:3
49. See Acts 2:38, 8:22
50. See Acts 17:30, 26:20
51. See II Corinthians 5:17 and Romans 6:23
52. Stephen Smalley, "Conversion in the New Testament," THE CHURCHMAN, Vol. 78, No. 3, pp. 193-210.
53. See I Peter 3:15
54. I Corinthians 3:6,8
55. See Ephesians 4:12
56. Charles Arn, Donald McGavran, Win Arn, *Growth: A New Vision for the Sunday School* (Pasadena: Church Growth Press, 1980), p. 129.
57. Flavil R. Yeakley, Jr., *Why Churches Grow* (Arcada: Christian Communications, 1979), p. 37.
58. Flavil R. Yeakley, Jr., "Research for the Growing Church," CHURCH GROWTH: AMERICA, January/February 1981, p. 10.
59. Arthur Glasser, *Why Church Growth* (Christian Communication: Part 2, N.D.).
60. Paul E. Little, op. cit., p. 53.
61. Win Arn, "A Church Growth Look at 'Here's Life America,' " *The Pastor's Church Growth Handbook* (Pasadena: Church Growth Press, 1979), pp. 44-60. Also, see C. Peter Wagner, "Who Found It?", ETERNITY, Vol. 28, No. 9.
62. Samuel Southard, *Pastoral Evangelism* (Atlanta: John Knox Press, 1981), p. 27.
63. Keith Miller, *Living the Adventure* (Waco: Word Press, 1975), p. 102.
64. See I Corinthians 3:6,8

Your Church— Partner in Disciple- Making

Christ desires that the Good News be proclaimed by His Church. Paul writes to the Ephesians, "That the manifold wisdom of God might be made known through the church in accordance with the eternal purpose which he carried out in Christ, Jesus our Lord."[1]

The church is absolutely essential to the disciple-making process. The church is not a Body of Christ, it is *the* Body of Christ; not just a bride of Christ, but *the* bride of Christ. The church is the central part of God's plan for making His Good News known.[2]

"The church is much like a movie projector that may be in or out of focus," observes Dr. George Peters in his book *A Theology of Church Growth.* "Its objective is to accomplish the purpose of God. Its concern must be to focus clearly on this purpose and then carefully, wisely pursue that goal. What is God's purpose? It broke through in full radiance and glory in the miracle of incarnation, the sending forth of His only begotten Son to be the Savior of the world and to reconcile that world to God."[3]

In your plans for reaching the members of your Extended Family, your church can play a more significant role than you ever imagined. It can increase immeasurably your effectiveness in communicating the Good News to your friends and relatives, and bring a unique resource to helping these people come into active, responsible church membership. Actually, disciple-making in *The Master's Plan* cannot occur without the active participation of the local church. The church is as important to effective disciple-making as any other single element. What do we mean?

Church-Centered Disciple-Making

The central role of the church in making disciples is based on an important concept in *The Master's Plan for Making Disciples*. The concept is called "church-centered disciple-making."

CHURCH-CENTERED DISCIPLE-MAKING—An intentional strategy and priority of the church which initiates disciple-making, trains members in disciple-making, uses resources of the Body, creates support resources, and incorporates new believers into the church.

Church-centered disciple-making puts the church—as a corporate Body—at the center of the evangelism process. It includes the church as a major partner in the disciple-making endeavor. Here are seven important contributions the local church makes to effective disciple-making:

1. *The church's ministry—instilling a "Great Commission conscience" in its members and organizations.*

A "Great Commission conscience" is the conviction among members that their church has the mandate, opportunity, and responsibility to communicate the Gospel to those who have yet to believe. In the church with a Great Commission conscience, a disciple-making mentality permeates every facet and organization of its Body. The result is a genuine concern by each member for friends, relations, and neighbors outside of Christ. A Great Commission conscience is fostered and kindled by church leaders who exhibit enthusiasm and devotion to making disciples, and constantly hold the disciple-making goal up as

The church's ministry—equipping its members to participate in the Great Commission.

a priority of the church's reason for being.

A Great Commission conscience is developed through preaching and Bible study focused on God's unswerving purpose to reach lost mankind. It is created as members are clearly taught the biblical foundations of caring for and reaching people outside of Christ. It is taught in Sunday School classes, small group fellowship meetings, in women's circles, in home cell groups. It is reflected and modeled in the lives of church officers, boards, committees, men's groups, women's groups, and youth groups. It is a "philosophy of ministry" which permeates the entire life of the church. A Great Commission conscience means that the entire church, and all of its parts, thinks and acts in response to the Great Commission.[4]

2. *The church's ministry—equipping its members to participate in the Great Commission.*

Church leaders have a scriptural mandate to equip the saints for the work of ministry: "God's people will be equipped to do better work for Him, building up the church, the Body of Christ, to a position of strength and maturity; until finally we all believe alike about our salvation and about our Savior, God's Son, and all become full-grown in the Lord—yes, to the point of being filled with Christ."[5]

The education ministry of your church is a natural place to help members understand the meaning of their faith, how to communicate their witness, the basic convictions of the Gospel, and how to point a friend to Christ. Peter's words are crystal clear: "Be always ready to account for the hope that is within you."[6]

Helping each member identify and use his/her spiritual gift(s) is another task of the church in equipping members to fulfill the Great Commission. Every member does not have the gift of evangelism, yet each Christian does possess a spiritual gift(s) that can be used in the disciple-making endeavor. The church with a Great Commission conscience uses *all* of the gifts of its members to communicate God's love to others. Spiritual gifts are a means to an end, not an end in themselves. The gifts of the Body are to be used in harmony with God's unswerving purpose for His Church and His people—the redemption of lost mankind.[7]

"You would misuse Christ's gifts if you used them solely for service of existing Christians. That is not why these gifts are given. As we see God's overwhelming concern for the salvation of people, we must assume that His gifts are given, at least in large part, that the lost may come to know Him."[8]

3. *The church's ministry—helping members develop plans and strategies to reach their Extended Family.*

The most natural and most responsive place to begin disciple-making in your church is within each member's own web of influence. Members of Sunday School classes, home Bible groups, sports teams, deacons, ushers can all begin to focus on the people in their web, and develop plans for seeing them come to Christ and the Church.

The local church body has the unique opportunity to help members see that making disciples is the concern of each

Christian, and that God has given each person a unique opportunity to share His love with certain people.

4. *The church's ministry—providing motivation, encouragement and accountability for members' disciple-making efforts.*

Members are most effective in disciple-making when the church structures regular encouragement, guidance, and accountability into the process. An important part of this support is providing opportunities for regular meetings to report progress, share triumphs, and relate experiences. Such church-sponsored "Support Team" groups encourage members in their commitment. As each member of the Support Team shares his/her disciple-making goals and concerns, members together feel an important sense of community in their task.

SUPPORT TEAM—A group of church members involved in making disciples who meet together regularly to encourage one another and learn how to more effectively communicate God's love to their Extended Family members.

The church can also provide encouragement as it publicly and personally affirms members in their disciple-making efforts. Regular support and visibility of members' disciple-making successes shows that it is significant in the eyes of church leadership, and basic to the goals of the congregation.

5. *The church's ministry—complementing members' disciple-making efforts.*

As we saw earlier, when non-Christians have a variety of opportunities to hear the Gospel and see it demonstrated, there is a much greater likelihood that they will eventually become active disciples. The church is a unique resource where Extended Family members can see the Christian faith demonstrated in a variety of settings, by a variety of people. Programs and activities of the church, such as music performances, recreation and sporting events, special-interest groups, mission presentations, church school learning experiences can creatively exemplify God's love and provide those varieties of exposures. Interaction between Extended Family members and church members is an important part of a successful disciple-making plan.

In his dissertation study, Dr. Flavil Yeakley analyzed the differences between the decision process of people who continued as active Christian disciples, and those who soon dropped out. He concluded that "when a person has no meaningful contact with the congregation in the process of his conversion, he is likely to feel no meaningful sense of identification with the congregation after his conversion and therefore he is likely to drop out."[9] Every opportunity for non-Christians to rub shoulders with church members provides an additional personification of Christ's love. Outsiders catch the warm, caring spirit. They sense the reality of Christ's presence that affects lives.

6. *The church's ministry—meeting needs of Extended Family members.*

A church effectively supporting member's disciple-making activities will plan programming and services designed around the needs and interests of Extended Family members. Focusing on such areas as perhaps single parents, seniors, young married couples, single young adults can present opportunities for relevant programs and activities where God's love can be experienced in caring and appropriate ways.

How does a church discover the needs and concerns of Extended Family members, so as to plan appropriately? The simplest way is often to ask individual members involved in the disciple-making process. As church members identify and strengthen their relationships with the members of their Extended Family, they naturally become aware of the interests, concerns, life situations, moments of stress of these people. Or, Lyle Schaller makes the comment, "If you want to find out people's needs, ask them."[10] Communication lines must be kept open between church leaders able to influence programming and members looking to respond to the needs of their Extended Family members.

The time-honored slogan "Find a need and fill it" has direct application for the church concerned with helping members make disciples. In finding needs of Extended Family members, the church discovers opportunities to meet those needs and share God's love as expressed through Jesus Christ.

7. *The church's ministry—organizing and administering the disciple-making process.*

"Without a vision, the people perish."[11] Churches eager to help members discover their hidden disciple-making potential have little problem with morale and involvement as the process begins to flourish. But for those dreams to become a reality, there are important administrative responsibilities to be carried out.

Personnel are necessary to coordinate disciple-making strategy and help implement each step. Making disciples may require "clearing the decks" of competing interests until the process becomes firmly established among groups and individual members in the church.

The commitment to making disciples will be reflected in the church budget. Adequate financial support of programs for disciple-making will really determine whether the church is sincere in supporting its members. Money on the line means the matter is serious.

Evaluation is an important part of administering the disciple-making process. Church leaders should regularly examine whether the church's disciple-making efforts are bringing fruit by looking closely at their own experience, other member's experience and actual results. Through regular evaluation, refinements in strategy can be made to build on the strengths and eliminate the problems. Evaluation should focus on the training process in disciple-making, member involvement levels, church support activities, and incorporation effectiveness.

Your Church's "POTENTIAL CONGREGATION"

Here is a powerful concept that will help translate "church-centered disciple-making" into a natural part of your church's planning and activities. It is a concept that should soon become a way of thinking for every church leader, officer, and staff member. The concept: your "Potential Congregation."

POTENTIAL CONGREGATION—The cumulative group of your church members' Extended Families.

Let's take a closer look at the idea of your church's Potential Congregation since it has important implications to the success of every church member's plan for reaching his/her Extended Family.

Disciple-Making Through
Your Church's Potential Congregation

The records in your church presently identify a group of individuals and families who comprise the "members of your congregation." These people are listed in the church directory, and are people about whom various information is kept. Perhaps their participation in church events is recorded. Most of the activities, programs, and classes planned by church leaders are done so with this group of members in mind. Most church leaders rightly feel that a major function of the church is to care for these members, to be responsive to their needs, and to provide a unique opportunity through the church for personal and spiritual growth. That is good, and the way it should be. Building up the Body is a significant function of the church.

Now consider the implications to your church's ministry if the definition of the "members of your congregation" were expanded. While the responsibilities for service to members would be the same, the "membership" of the congregation would now include new people . . . all those people, in fact, in the Extended Family of your present members. It is this group of people that form your church's Potential Congregation. They are quite winnable and waiting to be won.

In so re-defining its "congregation," your church enlarges and extends considerably its view of ministry. Your church's concern now extends beyond its present members to include all these potential disciples. Now you are not only serving existing members—who might be called your "Worshiping Congregation" but as a church you are responding to and ministering to those who make up your Potential Congregation as well. And, like the members of your Worshiping Congregation, the members of your Potential Congregation can be identified by name, information can be gathered on each, needs identified, and programs developed.

When You Identify Your Potential Congregation . . .

What is the impact of such a new view of your church and congregational responsibilities? How will this new view of disciple-making affect your church's outreach strategy and planning?

Here are six important implications:

1. *Your church, when it identifies its Potential Congregation, focuses on a specific and identifiable group of winnable people.*

The members of your Potential Congregation are people outside the Body of Christ, *but* people inside the Extended Families of present members; therefore they are very closely related to your church. The people within your church's Potential Congregation are significantly more reachable and winnable than those not in the web of present members.

A follow-up study to a recent Billy Graham Crusade shows the importance of focusing on winnable people.[12] The study, conducted one year following the crusade, looked for the people who had made a decision during the course of the event to find out how many were then involved in a local church. It turned out that only fifteen out of every 100 people who came forward for a decision could later be found participating in a local church. However, of those people who were active, *eighty-two percent* had a friend or relative in that church *prior* to their decision! A great majority of the new converts found in churches one year later had actually been in the Extended Family of a church member, and part of that church's Potential Congregation. The prior relationship with the church member had provided the "bridge" for the new Christian to come into the church, and provided the "glue" to keep that new believer incorporated.

An additional study underscores the fact that friends and relatives are a key in the process of making a religious decision. The Mormon sect keeps accurate records of the successes and failures of its mission endeavors. A study published in the American Journal of Sociology[13] reports that the "success rate" of the Mormon missionaries, who go from door to door calling, is approximately .1% (one conversion per 1,000 contacts). However, when these same missionaries present the Mormon message in the home of one of their church members to a non-Mormon neighbor, the success rate jumps to fifty percent! The article "How to Share the Message with Your Neighbors" published in their national magazine exemplifies their strategy of encouraging relationships between members and neighbors to convert new people to their beliefs.[14]

2. *Your church, when it identifies its Potential Congregation, focuses its caring ministry.*

Caring is a beautiful and important function of the Body of Christ. Too often however people have to be on the "inside" to experience it. In your Potential Congregation an exciting new possibility opens to your church. Caring continues to be a major function in the life of the congregation, and is still focused on the needs and concerns of its present members. However, this caring is now also extended to the members of your Potential Congregation and opens an important new group of people as recipients to the church's concern. The need to be cared for and loved is a need common to all individuals. The church that focuses its caring ministry on both present members and potential members will see significant results as those in the Potential Congregation respond to this caring and become new disciples. The church is exemplifying the love of God in His name.

3. *Your church, when it identifies its **Potential Congregation**, focuses programming to meet needs.*

Most ministries in a church are planned for the members of that congregation. The "youth ministry" is for the youth in the church. The "music ministry" is generally for the benefit and involvement of members in the church. The "minister of education" is paid to organize Christian education to nurture church members.

A Potential Congregation will help your church evaluate and prioritize its programming efforts. While programming and ministry are still focused on the needs and interests of members, the expanded definition of "members" now means programming and planning considerations include Potential Congregation members as well. Of course every event in the church is not expected to focus on both groups. But over the course of the church year, there should be equal consideration given to each group in the overall planning, development, and appropriation of church resources.

In the planning of programs, special events, and seminars, the unique needs and interests of members in your church's Potential Congregation should be carefully considered. Because the needs and interests of non-Christians differ, don't assume that all members of your Potential Congregation will respond to one type of programming. Just as every member of your Worshiping Congregation would probably not be interested in the women's brunch, or the young married's class, or the single's retreat, potential disciples will have a variety of interests as well. In planning ministry to your Potential Congregation, take into account the unique qualities of these potential disciples.

They have special concerns and interests, family situations, certain images of the church and its people. It is around the unique needs of both Worshiping Congregation members and Potential Congregation members that your church should concern itself in planning for effective ministry.

4. *Your church, when it identifies its **Potential Congregation**, experiences increased morale.*

A minister of evangelism recently recalled to us the tremendous change in morale as a result of a successful outreach strategy in their church to friends and relatives. "At first, when the new members were presented to the congregation for baptism," he recalled, "most people in the church didn't quite know what to do. It had been a long time since that many people had joined the church at one time. But as the months went on, and more friends and relatives began coming to Christ and the church, it really started to sink in. Older members began to believe that maybe the church did have something to offer outsiders. As they heard the new Christians testify to the joy and excitement of their new faith, it really turned a lot of attitudes around. It's been like a snowball picking up momentum as it rolls down the hill . . . it just keeps building on itself!"

Contagious enthusiasm and excitement invariably results when members see their long-time friends and relatives come into new life in Christ and their church. Morale level also builds as the new Christians, who are invariably enthusiastic about their new-found dimension to life, become active in the church. Making disciples and reaching the members of your Potential Congregation can uncover new dimensions of spiritual growth and vitality which you may never have thought existed in your church.

5. *Your church, when it identifies its **Potential Congregation**, more effectively invests its resources.*

An obvious concern of church leadership is good stewardship of resources. Poor stewardship invests the church's time, money, and most valuable commodity—people—in areas that do not produce a return. Yet, as we saw at the beginning of this book, much time and many people are being invested in methods of evangelism that do not result in comparable "harvest." This does not happen when resources are invested and focused on a church's Potential Congregation. These potential disciples have been identified as one of the most receptive groups of people in your community. It is simply good stewardship to respond to the people God has prepared, and do our part in bringing them into the Kingdom.

Because your church has identified these specific groups of people (members' Extended Families) to whom you seek to communicate God's love, you can accurately evaluate the effectiveness of various ministries in terms of new Christian disciples. Some approaches and programs for these people will be more effective than others. Effective strategy should be based on the ministries that bring results.

6. *Your church, when it identifies its Potential Congregation, experiences a continually expanding congregation.*

As members of your Potential Congregation make a commitment to Christ and become members of the Body and the Worshiping Congregation, they each have their own web of influence. As these new disciples are helped in their disciple-making plans, they identify members in their Extended Family and, as a result, increase the size of the Potential Congregation. And so the process begins all over again. This is exactly the way the early church grew . . . first by addition,[15] then by multiplication.[16]

▶◀▶◀▶◀▶◀

The various Support Team Members had been taking turns hosting the bi-weekly meetings. Chuck and Diane arrived at Bob Odman's apartment and spent a few minutes in informal fellowship before Tim, the Team Coordinator, convened the meeting.

One by one the various members shared what had been happening in their disciple-making endeavors since their previous meeting. Steve told about his cousin he was focusing on and how they had gone out for a hamburger one evening last week. "We didn't talk about religion or anything," Steve said. "But we're starting to get to know each other a lot better. We've shared some personal feelings and there's a good level of trust building."

"Sounds encouraging," Tim said. "Have you introduced your cousin to anyone else in the church?"

"No, I guess I should do that," Steve reflected. "Let's see now . . ."

"How about the softball team?" asked Diane Bradley. "Does he like softball?"

"No, he's more of an intellectual type. He wouldn't go for those simple, mundane things." Steve looked over at Bill, the pitcher on the softball team.

"Hey!" retorted Bill, "Softball is a real intellectual activity. Not everyone can play, you know."

"Does he like chess?" asked Sue.

"Yeah, he loves it. But do any of you guys play chess?"

"No," said Chuck. "But, you know, maybe the church ought to have a chess league. It might be a neat thing to invite our Extended Family members to who like chess."

"That would be a great way to introduce them to other people in the church, too," added Steve.

"Good idea. I'll make a note of that and talk to Dave Johnson about it," said Tim, referring to the associate pastor of the church.

After the discussion about Steve's cousin, another member of the group, spoke up. "As you know, I've been working with two people in my web—my sister Helen, and my next door neighbor Jim Herman. To tell you the truth, I'm kind of frustrated. It seems like nothing much has been happening in the last couple months; particularly with my neighbor."

"What seems to be the problem?" asked Tim.

"Well, you see, I don't have much in common with him."

"I know what you mean," said Chuck. "When I was focusing on my neighbor Pete, all he ever talked about was fishing. I hate fishing. I almost gave up. But one time I

*brought Andrew along. He loves fishing. Well, he and Pete hit
it off pretty well. Maybe you could introduce your neighbor to
someone in the church that might have more in common
with him."*

*"He does have a thing about gardening, especially flowers.
Tim, you play in the dirt, don't you?"*

*"Well, I enjoy gardening, if that's what you mean," said
Tim. "You know there's a horticultural show down at the
center next week. Why don't I stop by and see if he wants to
go? You ought to go along too, though."*

"Sure, I'll go."

*The meeting went on another thirty minutes, with other
members sharing the progress of their disciple-making efforts
and talking through additional plans for communicating
God's love to each Extended Family member. Some of the
members reported real progress, while others had to be
encouraged to "wait on the Lord."*

*Tim then led the group in a fifteen-minute Bible study.
They had been studying various personalities in the New
Testament and how each had responded to the Great
Commission. This particular evening they were studying
about the Apostle Barnabas.*

*Following the Bible study, Tim passed out copies of a
sheet listing upcoming church-sponsored activities which
might be appropriate for members to use in their disciple-
making plans. The sheet listed various sports events, social
outings, and seminars which had all been designed to be part
of the church's disciple-making support strategy.*

*The group concluded with prayer for each Extended
Family member mentioned that night, and then set the time
and place for the next Support Team meeting.*

Footnotes

1. Ephesians 3:10-11
2. Win Arn, *The Pastor's Church Growth Handbook* (Pasadena: Church
   Growth Press, 1979), p. 54.

3. George W. Peters, *A Theology of Church Growth* (Grand Rapids: Zondervan Publishing House, 1981), p. 240.
4. *The Master's Plan Church Action Kit* has excellent and specific ideas to raise the disciple-making awareness of laity in a local congregation. Information on The Master's Plan Church Action Kit is available from the Institute for American Church Growth, 709 E. Colorado Blvd., Suite #150, Pasadena, California 91101
5. Ephesians 4:12-13
6. I Peter 3:15
7. David L. Hocking, *The World's Greatest Church* (Long Beach: Grace Ministries, 1976), p. 36.
8. Donald A. McGavran and Win Arn, *How to Grow a Church* (Glendale: Regal Books, 1973), p. 36.
9. Flavil R. Yeakley, *Why Churches Grow* (Arvada: Christian Communications, 1979), p. 66.
10. Interview with Rev. Robert Orr and Lyle Schaller, January, 1977, Pasadena, California.
11. Proverbs 29:18
12. Win Arn, "Mass Evangelism: The Bottom Line," CHURCH GROWTH: AMERICA, January/February 1978, p. 4.
13. Rodney Stark and William Sims Bainbridge, "Recruitment to Cults and Sects," AMERICAN JOURNAL OF SOCIOLOGY, Vol. 85, No. 6, pp. 1376-1395.
14. Ernest Eberhard, "How to Share the Gospel," *The Ensign*, June 1974, pp. 6-11.
15. See Acts 2:47
16. Acts 6:7

Incorporating New Disciples into the Church

This was the night for paying monthly household bills. Those who knew Chuck well, like his wife, Diane, and his daughter, Karen, made it a point to avoid the den that entire evening. To make matters worse, Chuck's calculator had expired with only half the bills paid.

Then the phone rang. Chuck didn't even make a pretense about hiding his frustration. The caller was Mary, his sister.

Diane walked by the door just as the phone rang and looked in to see an amazing sight. Chuck, despite his state of frustration, was smiling! And what was more unusual, there were tears in his eyes.

A very curious Diane broke her long-standing rule and entered Chuck's den on billpaying night to find out what was going on.

Chuck hung up the phone, turned to Diane and continued to smile.

"Sweetheart, that was Mary, my sister. She's just recommitted her life to Christ and she's going to join the church."

Diane gave her husband a warm hug. "And to think that just a little over a year ago you were insisting you couldn't possibly be a witness!"

"Well, Diane, much as I hate to admit, I guess I was wrong."

Chuck, despite his state of frustration, was smiling! And what was more unusual, there were tears in his eyes.

"Chuck, did I hear you say you were wrong? Now that is hard to believe."

Another phone call saved Chuck from having to respond. It was Pastor Austin.

"Yes, Pastor, she did call. Yes, I do understand my responsibility for both of them."

What Pastor Austin was reminding Chuck about was the vital importance of new disciples like Pete and Mary being successfully incorporated into the church.

"Unless they become responsible members of the church," the Pastor had rightly said, *"and assume their own place in the Body, the disciple-making process is incomplete."*

It is true. Evangelism is not complete without the new Christian becoming an active part of the church. There are some important things to remember about the process of incorporating a new member. Consider Mary, for example . . .

Incorporation—Some Assumptions

1. *Mary's incorporation will not be automatic.* Laity often assume that newcomers to the church will naturally look for and find a place in one group or another, and be immediately accepted by members of that group. As the old saying goes, "It ain't necessarily so." It is often surprisingly difficult for a newcomer to find a place where he/she fits and finds a sense of belonging. Most groups do not automatically reach out and incorporate the outsider. As a result there is often a high mortality rate among new Christians. The importance of caring for and nurturing the new believer is reflected in the analogy of a new baby requiring much care and feeding and special attention. Just as the new baby cannot survive without the help of others, the new Christian needs the special help of others to begin his/her new life.

2. *The church, rather than Mary, is responsible for her incorporation into the Body.* The vast majority of new Christians join a church with the expectation of growing into active and contributing members. They want to learn, and grow, and build meaningful relationships in their new church home. If they never become active church members, the problem usually can be traced to the church rather than the new member. Monitoring the new Christian's involvement in the church, particularly during the first few critical months, should be a regular practice of the church body and its various organizations. If new Christians drop out of a church, in most cases the church has failed in its responsibility.

3. *The people who brought Mary to Christ have the primary responsibility to help her become an active member.* Friends or relatives already in a church make all the difference in the world for incorporating that new member into the church. When the new Christian sees familiar faces in this new environment, and has friends who help him/her build new relationships with others, assimilation takes place much more naturally.

4. *Mary's incorporation began before membership.* The incorporation process of a new disciple actually starts long

before the person joins the church. The friendships
established with others in the church earlier in the disciple-
making process now serve as a natural bridge into the
Worshiping Congregation. Extended Family members, who
earlier became part of a group in the church, are actually
incorporated before they formally join. According to Lyle
Schaller, among those not related to a congregation by
kinship, those most likely to remain active have become part
of a small group where membership in that group was
important before formally uniting with that congregation.
They are assimilated before they join.[1]

   5. *Mary's incorporation must be a high priority for the
church.* There is no great accomplishment in fulfilling the
Great Commission if people coming in the "front door" of
the church are exiting out the "back door" in equal numbers.
A commitment of time, money, and people is necessary for a
church to have an effective incorporation strategy, and for
Extended Family members to find a place they can call
home. Providing for the development and growth of new
members and equipping them for ministry are necessary
steps in making disciples.

The Incorporation of Extended Family Members—
A Church-Centered Strategy

   How do we insure that new Christians and church
members become integrated into the life of the
congregation, that they develop a sense of belonging and
identity and become an active part of the church's life and
ministry?

   The question of incorporation is crucial. A strategy
for successful incorporation of new members is a major part
of any church's commitment to making disciples. A church-
centered approach to incorporation rightly assumes the
centrality of the church in this process.

   Here are five steps to seeing an effective incorporation
strategy become a reality in your church . . .

1. Build an "incorporation consciousness." A church with an incorporation consciousness is one where people go out of their way to greet the newcomer and get to know him/her; where they do everything possible to make the person feel welcome and an important part of the church. In most churches, however, an "incorporation consciousness" does not naturally occur. And while many congregations like to think of themselves as a "friendly church," a first-time visitor might have quite a different impression. Often smaller groups in a church, without realizing it, actually exclude and even isolate newcomers. A conscious and continuous effort must be made, therefore, to encourage laity and groups in the church to be open to outsiders.

Building an incorporation consciousness is not difficult. But it requires a high priority on the part of church leaders, officers, and members. Incorporation of new members should be a regular agenda item of most boards and officers meetings. Sunday School class sessions, small group meetings, worship services, and mid-week prayer meetings should frequently stress to each layperson the importance of being open and caring to the newcomer.

2. Develop an incorporation structure. More and more churches, seeing the need for a formal concern for the incorporation of new members, are establishing a committee on assimilation. Here are some suggestions for organizing a system for incorporation in your church:

- Establish a "new member tracking committee" of lay people exclusively concerned with overseeing the first nine months of the new member's life in the church. The committee keeps accurate records and updated information on every new member. It provides information to each class or small group when patterns of inactivity are discerned.
- Appoint a person in each class and small group in the church to be responsible for the incorporation of new people. Such a person is responsible to see that new people are introduced to others in the group, and that the

DO YOU HAVE
AN INCORPORATION PROBLEM?

Consider your own church and answer the following questions:

1. Are there large numbers of "transfers out" who keep the same residency?
2. Are there more than 50% of the people in your church with no specific role, task, or small group identification?
3. Is there a large gap between church membership and average worship attendance?
4. Is there a large gap between Sunday School enrollment and Sunday School attendance?
5. Is there a high percentage of the members whose worship attendance is one Sunday per month or less?
6. If you were to ask them, would many of the members feel "left out"?
7. Are there large numbers of visitors who do not come back?
8. Is there a high percentage of new members who have not been exposed to the ministries and people of your church prior to their joining?
9. Are there large numbers of new members who do not have a friend or relative in the church already?
10. Are there members whose level of involvement suddenly declines?
11. Are there needs among your members, which are appropriate for the church to meet, which are not being met?

If the answer to many of the questions is "yes," you may have an incorporation problem and should consider ways to go about solving it.

class or group is open to accept them.

- Research previous incorporation results. Analyze the present level of involvement of church members who have joined the church in the last two years. How many are now active church members, and how many have dropped out? Studying the patterns of incorporation gives unique insights into present strengths and weaknesses.
- Interview once-active, but now inactive, members to find out why they dropped out. Lessons learned from these people are valuable in alleviating potential problems for future new members.

3. Provide friendship-building opportunities. As we have seen, the number of close friends a new member develops in the church has a direct influence on whether he/she continues as an active member. If, after six months, the new member can identify few or no close friends in the church, the chances are extremely high that the person will soon be inactive. But if the new member has a growing number of close friends who are active in the church, it will be very unusual for that person to drop out. The "friendship factor," research tells us, is the most important element in whether a person remains active in a local church, or drops out.[2]

What does this mean for your church?

One implication is that church groups should provide opportunities for building friendships among members. Organize activities that are just plain fun! Activities that strengthen personal ties between members. Be sure that both old members and new members (and potential new members) are in attendance. The event should not be just a social occasion to entertain the same old gang.

An effective incorporation strategy will help new members build additional relationships beyond the friend/relative originally responsible for bringing the person to Christ. You will know your incorporation strategy is working when you see new members continue on as active members even when the original friend or relative moves to another city or goes on to be with the Lord.

4. Structure need-meeting ministries. A fourth step toward an effective incorporation strategy for new members centers on the unique needs which these people bring to the church . . . personal, spiritual, marital, occupational, relational. Life is full of problems. Becoming a Christian and member of a church does not mean all problems go away. But the Christian faith does provide a deep pool of strength from which to draw in coping with problems. A church concerned with seeing people grow and mature in the Christian life should have ministries that directly respond to the needs of its members—particularly its new members.

Starting new groups is an excellent way to provide such support. Groups or classes may be topically oriented and deal with certain areas of concern to members. A list of such need-meeting classes might look like this:

Personal
—How to reduce weight
—Stop smoking seminars
—Coping with stress
—Feeling good about yourself
—Self-discipline—why and how
Spiritual
—What the Bible says about _____
—How to share your faith with your friends
—Daily Bible study—why and how
—Discovering and using your spiritual gift/s
—Prayer: Is anyone listening?
Marital
—Communicating with your spouse
—Your marriage: the first 100 days
—New parents class
—Coping with divorce and remarriage
—Children and drugs
Occupational
—Dealing with job related anxiety
—Working in a non-Christian environment

—Re-entering the job market
—Changing jobs
Relational
—Learning to listen
—How to deepen your friendships
—Dating and the Christian
—Coping with in-laws

Obviously there are many others. And the ministries provided will vary according to age, marital status, personal interests, particular needs. The best way to identify appropriate groups or topics is to form an ad hoc committee responsible for identifying various areas of need to which the church can respond. If your Great Commission conscience is beginning to develop, you will see that such need-meeting ministries can not only serve the new members, but can also provide ideal opportunities to introduce yet-to-be-reached Extended Family members to the church and its people.

5. Create new roles and tasks. How many opportunities for role or task involvement presently exist in your church? In a typical church of 300 members there are approximately eighty such opportunities for laity to fill a role and/or task. Three-fourths of those present roles are usually filled by ten percent of the members (having several jobs each). The remaining roles are filled by additional members. So in the typical church of 300 members, 50 members are filling some kind of role or task, leaving 250 members with no role or task. This is a church structured for non-growth. Members who have no specific responsibilities couldn't get involved if they wanted to; there just aren't enough roles to go around.

There is a direct relationship between the number of roles or tasks available in a church, and the number of new people the church can incorporate. According to a recent study of churches effectively incorporating new people, an ideal ratio of roles to members is fifty-five per one hundred.[3] That is, for every one hundred adult members there should be at least fifty-five different roles or tasks available. The study also found that in churches with a high drop-out rate of new members, the ratio of roles to members was twenty-seven per one hundred, and often lower.

What does this principle of incorporation mean for your church?

One implication is that new roles and tasks should be created at the same, or greater, rate as the number of new members being added. These new roles and tasks should obviously be fulfilling and meaningful to the person involved. The new roles should also have a direct contribution to achieving the goals which the church has established. Providing specific responsibilities for new members can open to them challenging opportunities of service and ministry through the church—ministry that perpetuates and expands the disciple-making effectiveness of the total congregation.

6. Monitor incorporation results. A key and on-going part of effective incorporation involves monitoring new members' involvement in the church. Systematically observing worship attendance, Sunday School attendance, and involvement in small group meetings provides important clues as to the new member's feeling of satisfaction with his/her church life. Closely monitor the involvement levels of each new member for the first nine months of his/her life in the church. And respond immediately at the first sign of problems.

"Sure," you're probably saying. "That's nice in theory, but do you realize what that really means?"

Yes, it's a considerable undertaking. In fact, monitoring incorporation patterns is a job most churches do little or nothing about, simply because of the size of the task. Yet, doesn't it seem reasonable that if we are actually concerned with reaching people and making disciples, we should be equally concerned with seeing that these people are effectively incorporated into the life of the Body? Remember the first assumption about Chuck's sister Mary in the incorporation process: "It is not automatic."

So, how do you practically monitor the involvement of the new member?

Keep records of attendance in classes or smaller group functions. A designated attendance-taker can quickly tally members and visitors present, and later analyze patterns of participation. Worship attendance patterns are also important to watch. Studies show that fluctuating attendance at worship is the best barometer to indicate a person beginning the drop-out process.[4] Here are some suggestions of how churches monitor worship attendance:

- Each Sunday School class and small group in the church appoints a person responsible to check the worship attendance of members in their group. For those church members not involved in any small group, their names are assigned to other persons to check.

- Growing numbers of churches (and not just the 1000 + member churches) are finding name tags to have a valuable function in their worship service. Not only do name tags make it easier for newcomers to learn and remember names, they provide a creative way to check attendance at worship. Each week members pick up their name tags from a rack as they enter the church area (and leave them on the way out). During the service an usher records the badges that are still on the rack, and has a record of those not present (or those not wearing their name tags, which is almost as bad!).

- Many churches use pre-printed cards available in the pews. Members and visitors alike fill them out and drop them in the offering plate or pass them down the aisle.

- A clipboard passed down each aisle is an excellent way to encourage every person to indicate his/her attendance.

What do you do with your list of members who were not in church last Sunday?

If the person is a new member, and came into the church through the Extended Family of someone in the church, the best step is to communicate the situation to the original church member. He/she can then look into why the person was not in attendance. There may also be one or more people in the church who are on a friendly basis with the new member. Let them know about the situation and encourage them to find out the reason for the fluctuating involvement level. If there is no one in the church on such a friendly basis with the new member (which should give you a good indication of why he/she may be dropping out), encourage someone from a smaller group in the church, with a common interest or age, to call.[5]

A disciple of Jesus Christ is one who is active in the body of Christ, growing spiritually, and then identifying and reaching out to members of his/her Extended Family. The growing cycle of new disciples continues when new members become active and involved in the life of the local church. Incorporating new believers into the fellowship of the Worshiping Congregation should be an important priority of the church.

Characteristics of an Incorporated Member

Six months after his sister Mary had joined the church, Chuck was optimistic about her growing level of involvement and identification with the church. He had good reason to be, based on the way Mary conformed to the following nine characteristics of an incorporated member.

1. An incorporated member identifies with the goals of the church. A clear statement of the goals and priorities which the church holds as central to its purpose, will provide an important point for members—especially new members—to rally around. For many newcomers these goals are the only thing they have in common with other members. The specific goals of a church should: 1) be directed toward accomplishing the purpose for why the church exists, 2) be clearly measurable and achievable, and include events/activities that will reach those goals, 3) be communicated clearly to church members (especially new members), and 4) describe how people can become involved. The goals should be reviewed yearly. New members should be encouraged to become actively involved in and identified with one or more of these specific goals.

One of the first topics of the new members class which Mary was participating in concerned the stated philosophy and goals of the church. Pastor Austin presented the various statements of purpose and how the programs and ministries all related to those goals. He then explained the importance of each member's commitment to these directives through various opportunities for involvement.

2. An incorporated member is regular in worship attendance. Nearly everyone would agree that an active, responsible church member participates regularly in worship. For most Christians, Sunday morning is the focal point in the church calendar. It is that designated time when the people of God come together to worship Him and to strengthen the church-wide celebration of the Christian faith. A new Christian not participating in the worshiping life of the church is certainly missing a critical time of corporate and personal "feeding" and growing in the Word.

In the six months since Mary had committed her life to Christ, she had missed only one worship service. She had even taken part in several of the services, reading the Scripture and reporting on the "new neighbor outreach" program she was involved in.

3. An incorporated member feels a sense of spiritual growth and progress. It is important for every Christian to feel a sense of movement and spiritual growth. This is especially true for the new Christian who has so much to learn and know about this new life in Christ. Formal, as well as informal, Christian education should begin immediately. A special class for new Christians is always valuable in helping them understand their new faith.

*Chuck could see almost daily growth in Mary's spiritual
life. The Bible study group she was part of on Thursday
mornings was a big part of her week. Mary was enthusiastically involved in her Sunday School class, which was
studying Romans, and she was starting to tell Chuck things
she had learned in her study that even Chuck didn't know.*

**4. An incorporated member has taken necessary steps of
affiliation with the Body.** Different churches have different
formal procedures for officially welcoming a new member
into the fellowship. For some it is baptism. For others it is a
special service. In other churches, it's a time of personal
testimony to the congregation. Whatever that formal step
may be, it is important that the new Christian take it soon
after his/her Christian commitment, and thus officially identify
with the Body. Such a step gives the new Christian a sense of
beginning. It also gives the church Body formal notification
that a new member is in their presence and they should be
open and welcoming of that new member.

*Following her recommitment to Christ and instruction by
Pastor Austin on what it meant to be a Christian and member
of that church, Mary had been presented to the church for
membership and baptism. Following the service, she and
fourteen other new members were the guests of honor at a
church picnic. There Mary and the others each gave their
personal testimony of how they had come to Christ. Eleven of
the new members reflected how some person or persons in
the church had played an important part in their coming to
Christ and the church. It was an exciting and rewarding time
for everyone involved.*

**5. An incorporated member has new friends in the
church.** The number of new Christian friends a person
makes during the first six months of his/her church life
directly influences whether that person continues as an active
member, or drops out. The following chart, adapted from an

article in CHURCH GROWTH: AMERICA magazine,[6] compares 100 people who recently made a Christian decision, 50 who are now active in their church, and 50 who have since dropped out. The chart compares the number of friends each group made in the church during the first six months.

Number of New Friends in the Church	0	1	2	3	4	5	6	7	8	9+
Actives	0	0	0	1	2	2	8	13	12	12
Drop-outs	8	13	14	8	4	2	1	0	0	0

Notice the striking difference between the number of new friends the active members could identify (for example, 13 of the now active members could identify 7 new friends, 12 active members could identify 8 new friends, 12 could identify 9 or more). Compare this to the group who dropped out and the number of new friends they made in the church. In overview, the average active member could identify over seven new friends in the church, the drop-outs only two.

The 2000 member Lake Avenue Congregational Church (Pasadena, CA), in seeking to provide for these important relationships, has identified a major function of their Christian education classes, and written it in their philosophy of ministry statement: "They are to function relationally, as congregations, providing the necessary feeling of belonging and togetherness, providing social functions appropriate for each age level, providing social concern and practical care for the members."[7]

After three months Mary could name five new friends she felt close to and went out with regularly. After six months she could identify nine new friends in the church, and she was beginning to feel quite comfortable in the groups and meetings in which she participated.

6. An incorporated member has a task or role

appropriate to his/her spiritual gift/s. A "role" is an officially appointed or elected position for a person in the church, such as serving on an ad hoc committee, a board, welcoming visitors, leading a Bible study. A "task" is a special, goal-oriented assignment, such as helping with the planning of a church worship service, helping to repave the parking lot, working on a special missions project.

The more roles available to be filled, the more members can be involved. Once the roles have been created, church leaders' responsibility is to effectively assign roles to people with an appropriate spiritual gift. A wide variety of resources are available today to help members discover their spiritual gift/s.[8] As older members and newer members begin to discover their spiritual gifts, they are invariably drawn to tasks for which God has equipped them.

Mary had accepted the role of incorporation coordinator in her Sunday School class. It was her duty to be the first to greet visitors who came to the class. She would learn their names and introduce them to others in the class. Mary had also participated in a Spiritual Gifts discovery course and found she had the gift of hospitality. So she had become part of a "new neighbor" program in the community where church members invite those who are just moving into the community to their house for dinner. Mary is enjoying her new roles and feeling fulfilled as a contributing member of the church.

7. An incorporated member is involved in a fellowship group. One of the most meaningful, rewarding, growing experiences the new Christian will experience is in a smaller group of the church where the caring, loving fellowship of the Body can be experienced. This small group involvement should be one of the first concerns of the church for its new members.

Organizing and regularly starting new groups for new members can be an effective strategy of incorporation. Often

a new member will become active in a new group, as a
"pioneer," where it might be difficult for him/her to break into
an existing group where relationships are already established.

*Mary fit easily into the Sunday School class where her
two other friends were already members. She had even met
several others in the class before, from previous church
events she had attended. Mary also enrolled in the new
members class and now six other new members and she
were meeting for Bible study every Thursday morning.*

**8. The incorporated member regularly tithes to the
church.** "Where your treasure is there will your heart be also."[9]
An important part of any member's responsibility to the
church is financial. Regular stewardship should be stressed
as a part of commitment to Christ and the church.

*Mary is not wealthy, but she has been faithfully tithing
each month since she joined the church.*

**9. The incorporated member is participating in the Great
Commission.** A disciple of Jesus Christ is one who is actively
involved in spreading the Good News to the members of his/
her Extended Family. New Christians are some of the most
enthusiastic people in the world. Many have just turned
around 180° in their lifestyle, and are so positively excited
with their new faith that their enthusiasm results in a natural
pattern of friends and relatives coming to Christ and the
church over a very short period of time. This natural desire to
tell others should be encouraged.

*One of the last topics in Mary's new member class was
the importance of disciple-making as a part of Christ's call.
Pastor Austin introduced the fact that each person has a
group of close friends and relatives who are "potential
disciples." Every person in the class was encouraged to
identify the people in their Extended Family and develop*

disciple-making plans for reaching them. Mary had identified Cheryl Riley, a neighbor in her next door apartment, as a person to focus on. Mary had already begun building a stronger relationship with Cheryl and had told her of the new life she had found.

An effective incorporation strategy for new members should go hand in hand with an outreach strategy to friends and relatives. Through study, evaluation, planning, and regular monitoring of the incorporation process in your church, significant new levels of growth and ministry will be realized where new Christians can find a home and a place to grow.

Footnotes

1. Lyle Schaller, *Assimilating New Members* (Nashville: Abingdon, 1978), p. 76.
2. W. Charles Arn, "The Friendship Factor," CHURCH GROWTH: AMERICA, May/June 1981, p. 13.
3. Flavil Yeakley, Jr., *Why Churches Grow* (Arcada: Christian Communications, 1979), p. 44.
4. John Savage, *The Apathetic and Bored Church Member* (Pittsford, NY: LEAD Consultants, 1976), p. 57.
5. A fascinating new development is emerging on the American church scene which has the potential for making such enormous record keeping responsibilities and analysis considerably easier. It is in the field of computer technology. The Institute for American Church Growth is pioneering specific church growth computer programs (including the problems and challenges of incorporation). One such program is designed to keep records of each person's participation at various events/activities, and then analyze the involvement level. At certain points, when the attendance of any one person at any specified event crosses a given "threshold" (that is, it drops below an acceptable level as determined by the church), an "action notice" is generated alerting church leaders to the potential problem. Such a creative approach to a traditionally difficult record-keeping problem allows a church to use the "impersonal" computer as a tool for more effective ministry. For additional information on church growth computer technology, write: Institute for American Church Growth, Dept. of Information Management, 709 E. Colorado Blvd., Suite #150, Pasadena, California 91101.
6. W. Charles Arn, op. cit.
7. "Lake Avenue Philosophy of Ministry," Lake Avenue Congregational Church, Pasadena, California.
8. An excellent self-study kit is available to work through the subject of spiritual gifts: SPIRITUAL GIFTS FOR BUILDING THE BODY. Available from the church growth offices in Pasadena.
9. Matthew 6:21

The Master's Plan—to the Ends of the Earth

It was already well into Saturday when Chuck finished servicing his car. What had started out as a simple lube and oil change at home, to save money, had turned into a horrendous task. Chuck was covered with grease from head to toe, and bone weary. But at last he had done it all himself.

He was looking forward to a nice hot shower and contemplating sleeping in on Sunday morning. It had been years since the last time he had missed church. But with The Master's Plan working so well, Chuck was anticipating some time off from disciple-making. After all, half of his Extended Family members were now disciples with Extended Families of their own.

The warm water felt good on his stiff aching muscles and he was giving himself a generous covering of soap lather when Diane called.

"It's Pastor Austin. He has to talk to you immediately. He has to leave in five minutes for an emergency at County Hospital, but he insists he has to talk to you first."

"But, Diane, I'm all covered with soap."

Well, that's how Chuck ended up standing in a puddle of soapy water by the kitchen phone, clothed in a soggy, soapy robe. He tried to sound cheerful.

"Yes, Pastor, what can I do for you?"

What had started out as a simple lube and oil change had turned into a horrendous task.

Pastor Austin was calling to make sure Chuck could attend a special committee meeting the following morning. The only time he could arrange, which was "convenient" for everyone involved, was 30 minutes prior to the early service. "It won't take long, but we've got to get moving in some new areas."

"But, Pastor, I thought now that things were going so well, that some of us 'old timers' at this disciple-making business could start taking things a little easier. After all, my Extended Family is half-discipled. Why, we've almost got the Great Commission fulfilled."

Pastor Austin gave what Chuck thought to be a surprising answer. "Well, Chuck, we're thankful for what's been done so far, but did you know that we have only just begun?"

"Pastor, what do you mean!"

"For one thing, all of us 'old timers' need to get additional members into our Extended Families. And then we need to be sure disciple-making becomes the concern of all groups in

Diane says he's discovered that disciple-making is one of the most rewarding aspects of the Christian life.

the church. Then, I'm starting to wonder if we don't need to think about sponsoring at least one new church. And, of course, there's always our overseas ministry. Well, Chuck, I've got to get to the hospital. See you in the morning."

The surprising thing was that Chuck didn't act the least bit upset with this unexpected change of plans. There are some that say Chuck Bradley isn't the same since he's been involved in The Master's Plan. Diane says he's discovered that disciple-making is one of the most rewarding aspects of the Christian life.

As long as there are people yet unreached, Christ's command to make disciples remains . . .

Steps for Expanding Disciple-Making

1. Utilize new Christians. If you have met a new Christian recently, you know that their enthusiasm and excitement with their new life in Christ is contagious. They are the happiest people in the world, and want the world to know. Life in Christ grants one a refreshingly new lease on life. So many older Christians have forgotten what it was like B.C. (before Christ).

As a church leader, how do you broaden your church's disciple-making endeavors? A natural place to begin is among the new converts. New Christians have many new contacts often denied to established members.

The diagram below illustrates a surprising, yet natural, phenomenon that occurs in every church. The circle represents the church. The pyramid represents the world. A person at the bottom of the pyramid represents a person who is in the world but outside the church.

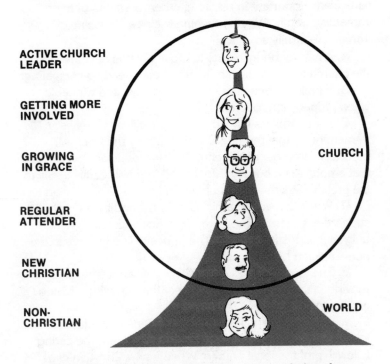

ACTIVE CHURCH LEADER

GETTING MORE INVOLVED

GROWING IN GRACE   CHURCH

REGULAR ATTENDER

NEW CHRISTIAN

NON-CHRISTIAN   WORLD

When the person becomes a Christian and church member, he/she still has a good number of contacts and

friends in the world. As time passes, however, the now older
Christian maintains fewer and fewer contacts in the world,
and more and more contacts in the church. The reason is
simply that as a Christian, he/she feels more comfortable
associating with other Christians. New life in Christ is not
often compatible with the lifestyle of old friends outside the
church.

Many growing churches have discovered the fact that new
converts have more contacts with unchurched prospects
than do long-time members. As a result, these churches
have found ways to effectively train the new Christians in how
to communicate the Good News to their friends.

Helping new Christians focus on their own webs is
particularly important in reaching other members of their
immediate family. Why is reaching the new Christian's
immediate family so critical?

A. A natural bridge exists to those outside of Christ and
the church through the family members already participating.

B. Family members are very responsive and winnable
when properly approached.

C. If the family is not won, the possibilities increase
tremendously that the one Christian family member will
eventually drop out of the church. Thousands of churches
that emphasize a bus ministry to children will readily testify to
the great losses that occur unless the entire family is won.

D. When the whole family is in Christ and the church, its
supportive system in the home provides encouragement,
unity, and Christian growth. The opposite is often true in the
non-Christian home.

E. The family itself is strengthened when all members are
moving in the same direction, rather than creating division
and fragmentation.

What attracts families and new persons to the faith is the
love of Christ, the moving of the Holy Spirit, and the caring
fellowship of the local church. When a new Christian can
express that power to his/her unreached family members, it
is an effective beginning to reaching the entire family.

2. Expand to all present groups in the church. Effective disciple-making does not stop with new Christians trained and involved in reaching out. Disciple-making does not stop with only one segment of the congregation trained or involved. *The Master's Plan* calls for every disciple of Christ to communicate God's love and caring to his/her own Extended Family.

As one accumulates experience in building a church-centered strategy of disciple-making, additional training sessions should begin. Those members who have been previously involved in *The Master's Plan* will be excellent references to help other members become God's source for communicating His love. The goal of disciple-making in the church should be to see every active member involved in communicating God's love and making disciples. This means helping each lay person identify the people in his/her Extended Family, to begin praying for them, caring for them, and planning to see these people come to Christ and the Church.

One way to facilitate the disciple-making process among older members is to help them build new relationships. We have stated that long time Christians usually have few contacts with non-Christians. But does this mean they are absolved of responsibility to reach new people? Of course not! But it does mean that a deliberate attempt may be needed to build new relationships with people outside of Christ.

CHURCH GROWTH: AMERICA magazine recently reported an example of the "web-building" process in action:

"The United Methodist Church in Carmel, Indiana, developed a strategy of identifying people who first move into its ministry area, and then building relationships between them and the church members. On a large map in the church, the community was divided into areas, sections, and sub-sections. One person or family from the church was assigned to a particular sub-section. (Members were assigned to a sub-section in which they lived.) Each sub-section was several blocks long. The members were then responsible for staying alert to any new people or families who moved into their sub-section. Members were encouraged to immediately introduce themselves to their new neighbors, welcome them, invite them to dinner, develop a friendship, and be alert to ways the church could respond and reach out to these new people. The program has been identified by church leaders as a major factor in the consistent growth of the church."[1]

3. Begin new groups. A third step in expanding the disciple-making process is to start new units. "New groups produce new growth."[2] Regularly starting new units (classes, groups, cells) significantly increases your church's effectiveness in disciple-making. In the book *Growth: A New Vision for the Sunday School,* eight reasons are given why new units should be regularly established:

1) New units provide a positive answer and response to the broad range of human needs.

2) New units are often more effective in incorporating people into a caring, belonging fellowship.

3) New units enlarge the church's appeal to new "kinds" of people.

4) New units are needed to replace those groups which have stagnated or have reached their maximum growth potential.

5) New units provide Christians with meaningful involvement and service opportunities.

6) New units discourage clustered, self-serving attitudes and programs.

7) New units are usually more effective in winning new people to Christ and the church.

8) New units help the "single cell" church begin the process of cell multiplication and growth.[3]

New groups should be designed with distinct appeal to certain "homogeneous" groups of people (newlyweds, young singles, senior singles, women re-entering the job market, widows, etc.). As more diverse groups become part of the

Here are nine simple steps to starting new groups in your church:

1) Define the target group of people to minister to.

2) Research the target audience and the kind of ministry that would possibly respond to their particular needs.

3) Find a committed lay person/s willing to be involved in starting such a new group. The person should be similar to the target group.

4) Train this person in the logistics of starting a new group.

5) Begin the recruiting process prior to the first group session.

6) Find an appropriate meeting place.

7) Stress the importance of the first several months. They are critical to the success of the group.

8) Keep accurate records of the experience for reference in starting later groups.

9) Build in monitoring and evaluation procedures for the first nine months.

church, new "kinds" of people will be able to find a home in the larger Body. Endeavor to match the new groups started with the variety of homogeneous kinds of people in your Potential Congregation and Worshiping Congregation. Any number of different kinds of people should be able to find a place in your church through becoming incorporated into a small, homogeneous group where they feel comfortable.

4. Start a new church. The "Great Commission Goal" is defined as: "a cell (church) of committed Christians in every community, in every city, and in every countryside throughout the world where people can hear and see demonstrated the Gospel by their own intimates, in their own tongue, and thus have a reasonable opportunity to become disciples of Jesus Christ."[4]

The Great Commission cannot be fulfilled in this country with the number of churches that presently exist. In fact, the 230,000 churches in America today could double without overchurching the country. Can this really be true when almost every community in America appears to be well-churched, with innumerable church buildings and open doors almost anywhere? One tends to conclude that there are plenty of churches in America, plenty of empty pews, and plenty of room for everyone. Such a conclusion needs to be challenged. While it may seem that there are enough churches for everyone, enormous numbers of people are unchurched and will remain so if we expect existing churches to reach them. The reason is that there are many people in America who simply will not feel comfortable in existing churches. Different churches appeal to different kinds of people. And there are segments of people in nearly every part of the country to whom no existing church provides attractive alternatives for their lives. Or, to say it another way, your church will not appeal to every person in your community, nor will any other.

The solution to this problem is not to hope other churches in the area will respond to the unique needs of these "unreachable" people. The secret is to identify who those people are and start a church deliberately structured to reach them.

The illustration below presents some important insights into both the cost and the effectiveness of disciple-making endeavors with various "homogeneous" groups of people in your community. The closer the group is to the center of the circle, the less costly and more effective disciple-making efforts will be by members of your church. The farther the groups are from the center circle, the more costly and less effective will be your disciple-making endeavors. By the time disciple-making efforts are focused on people in the far circles, the evangelism process has become one of "missions." And every good missionary knows that the most effective strategy is to win receptive people, plant a new church among those people, and then assist them in reaching their own families and webs. Such a new church, among this new group of people, changes the process of disciple-making from missions back to "near-neighbor" and returns to the center of the circle (resulting in greater effectiveness).

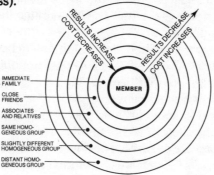

Many churches like to think of themselves in the pattern of the New Testament church, doing things in a biblical fashion. But is a church really a New Testament church if it isn't planting churches? Being a real New Testament church means believing and doing what the New Testament church did. The New Testament church was tremendously concerned with, engaged in, and *successful* at establishing new congregations. Churches were planted in Jerusalem, Judea, Samaria. Churches were planted in Galilee, Antioch, Rome, in city after city around the Mediterranean. Toward the end of his life, Paul was heading toward Spain to begin planting churches there. Church multiplication was an essential part of New Testament life. Today, in a world where three out of four persons have yet to believe in Jesus Christ, if a congregation is not reproducing, it is not a New Testament church, no matter what it calls itself.[5]

Church planting begins with the conviction that it is God's will that His Church grow. Such a conviction grows into a

deep concern for people in the community without Christ.
When these concerns permeate the people of God in the
local congregation, beginning a new church becomes a real
possibility.

Most churches discover that planting a daughter church
is not actually the drain of resources on the mother church
that perhaps they had thought it would be. Rather it often
proves to be a boost to growth, morale, and enthusiasm. Like
the birth of a new baby, a brand new congregation is a joy to
experience and be a part of.

If the vast mosaic of people in North America are going
to be reached for Christ, existing churches not only need to
grow themselves, but they need to give priority to the
multiplication of new churches.

Begin thinking about planned parenthood in your church
. . . why not one every nine months?

5. Reach across cultures. The Great Commission, which
Christ gave to His Church, was a command to disciple "to
the ends of the earth." Most English versions translate the
command of Christ in Matthew 28:19 to read: "make
disciples of all *nations.*" But this is a mistranslation. The
original Greek translation is to disciple "*ta ethne.*" "*Ethne*"
does not mean the modern nation states such as India, the
United States, or China. *Ethne* means the ethnic units of
mankind, all the mosaics and kinds of people in a nation, the
variety of levels and sub-cultures of society. The Great
Commission is a call to disciple every piece of the vast
mosaic of humankind which make up the three billion yet to
believe.[6]

In referring to his own call, Paul wrote: "This gospel . . . is
about Jesus Christ our Lord, through whom I received the
privilege of a commission . . . to bring to faith and obedience
men of all *ethne.*"[7] The Great Commission will be fulfilled
when every person has had a reasonable opportunity to see
and hear the Gospel from his/her own intimates, in his/her
own culture, and is given a chance to become part of a local
Body of Christ.

A church concerned with responding to the Great Commission will indeed direct its attention to the people in its Potential Congregation within its own community. But it will not be able to overlook the vast numbers of people yet to hear and yet to be reached beyond the perimeters of its own small part of the world.

Missions should have an important place in the priority of any church concerned with the Great Commission. A special missions coordinator or committee should be found in every church to frequently keep the world-wide task in front of the congregation. Regular sermons, Sunday School lessons, speakers, films, and reports on missions projects are valuable. Consider adopting a special missions project, if you do not have one. Encourage people in the church to visit that mission project. Perhaps sponsor a bi-annual church tour to the mission project and help raise money for members to go.

Christians, today, have the responsibility as no generation before to invest time, money, and people to reach out to "the ends of the earth" with the Good News.

Can the Great Commission be fulfilled?

We have come a long way since Christ left those few apostles with such a seemingly impossible task. There are now faithful Christians on every continent of the globe. There are Christian churches found in every country. It is not a question of *can* the Great Commission be fulfilled. It *is* being fulfilled. The question is whether you and your church will be a part. Will the Master return, as Christ illustrated in the parable of the talents, to find that your church has hidden its "treasure" and has nothing more to show? Or, will He return to find the treasure left in your care to be multiplied through faithful investment? And then will he say to you, "Well done thou good and faithful servant."

◆◀◆◀◆◀◆◀◆◀

Mark Peters and his friend Bob Taylor walked down the steps of the high school. It was a Friday evening. Mark and Bob had just finished playing in the church league basketball playoffs, helping their church to its first championship. They were exhilarated and exhausted as they headed toward their cars.

"Man, what a game!" reflected Mark.

"Yeah. What a season! Remember that first game?" laughed Bob.

"Don't remind me. Boy, did we get blown out of there."

"Well, we sure got our act together after that."

"You're coming to the celebration over at the church aren't you?" asked Mark.

"Well, I . . . I don't know," stammered Bob.

"Hey, come on," insisted Mark. "We couldn't have made it through the season without you."

"Well, okay. But I've got to get going soon."

"Great. I'll see you over there," said Mark as they each got in their car and left the parking lot.

Mark had been a member of the church for nearly a year. He had originally been introduced to Christ by his brother-in-law, Jim Herman. Jim, as it turned out, had been reached through a fishing buddy named Pete. And, of course, Pete was Chuck Bradley's first Extended Family member to come to Christ and the church.

So Mark was the fourth generation tracing his "spiritual roots" back to Chuck Bradley's involvement, over three years earlier, in the Master's Plan for making disciples. Even though they were in the same church, Chuck would probably never know that he had been indirectly responsible for Mark's own Christian commitment and involvement in the church. Or that Bob Taylor, now a member of Mark's own Extended Family, would soon respond to the caring of the church and the Body.

Since those first days of The Master's Plan, when Pastor Austin began meeting with various members and helping them share God's love with their Extended Family, the church had seen considerable new vitality and growth. In fact, a new committee had been organized during the previous week to examine the possibility of planting a new church in the coming year. The existing facilities were getting cramped and the church had already started holding a second service.

What had happened to this church in the last three years? How and why did it move from an "average" church, doing basically "average church work," to a dedicated and growing church, equipping its lay members to fulfill the Great Commission in their world?

The secret was in laity mobilized for making disciples. Chuck's church had discovered that the key to reaching their world for Christ was in lay people convinced: 1) of the opportunity that existed all about them, and 2) that they could individually, and as a church, expect to see their friends, relatives, and associates become Christians and members of their church.

It was not just because they had read a book, or participated in a special series of meetings. The reason Chuck's church began to realize its previously untapped possibilities, was because they had taken seriously important biblical insights, as well as modern day applications, of how Christ's Good News can be extended to the "uttermost parts of the earth." The laity had learned to communicate Christ's love and were using their natural networks for the expansion of His church.

Of course, there was not a 100% success rate. Not all the members of the church, who could have been, were involved in making disciples. Some Extended Family members never found Christ or His love through the church. A few new members that came into the church dropped out through oversights in the church incorporation system. But as Chuck, Pete, and several others on the church board were discussing at the last meeting, the events that took place three years previously, which launched the new emphasis in equipping laity and making disciples, had marked a significant new direction for the church. Those events had contributed directly to a new level of morale among the members, and the beginning of exciting new heights of achievement for the congregation in fulfilling Christ's command to go . . . and make disciples.

Footnotes

1. "Growing Ideas . . .", CHURCH GROWTH: AMERICA, January/February 1980, p. 15.
2. Charles Arn, Donald McGavran, Win Arn, *Growth: A New Vision for the Sunday School* (Pasadena: Church Growth Press, 1980), p. 105.
3. Ibid., p. 108.
4. *Basic Growth Seminar Workbook* (Pasadena: Institute for American Church Growth, 1979), p. 5.
5. Donald McGavran and Win Arn, *Ten Steps for Church Growth* (New York: Harper and Row, 1977), p. 96.
6. Ibid., p. 38.
7. Romans 1:1-5